I0815984
DUKE STREET
Property of the COLLEGE
COLLEGE GARDEN
Macfarlane Observatory
No. III
No. IV
No. VI
No. IX
No. X
No. VII
No. I
GALLOWGATE STREET
LONDON STREET
GREAT HAMILTON STREET
MONTEITH ROW
CATTLE MARKET
LOW GREEN
HIGH GREEN
EAST CLYDE STREET
ADELPHI STREET
GOVAN STREET
STONEFIELD the Property of ALEXR. WADDELL ESQR.
Property of the Heirs of Mr. WM. SCOTT
Property of HUTCHESON'S HOSPITAL
FLESHER'S HAUGH
New Burying Ground
Calton Burying Ground
REFERENCES to PARISHES.
No. I. Inner High Church Parish
II. St. Mary's Parish
III. Blackfriars Parish
IV. Outer High Church Parish
V. St. George's Parish
VI. St. Davids Parish
VII. St. Andrew's Parish
VIII. St. Enochs Parish
IX. St. Johns Parish
X. St. James Parish

Glasgow

A New History

Front endpaper: Plan of the City of Glasgow and its environs (1828) by David Smith (National Library of Scotland)
Back endpaper: W. and A.K. Johnston's Map of Glasgow (1927) drawn by A. Wilson (National Library of Scotland)

Glasgow

A New History

ALISTAIR MOFFAT

BIRLINN

First published in 2025 by
Birlinn Limited
West Newington House
10 Newington Road
Edinburgh
EH9 1QS

www.birlinn.co.uk

ISBN: 978 1 78027 958 9

British Library Cataloguing-in-Publication Data
A catalogue record for this book is available from the British Library

Typeset by Hewer Text UK Ltd, Edinburgh
Map by Helen Stirling

Papers used by Birlinn Ltd are from well-managed forests and other responsible sources

Printed and bound by CPI Group (UK) Ltd, Croydon, CRO 4YY

For George Rosie

Contents

Map

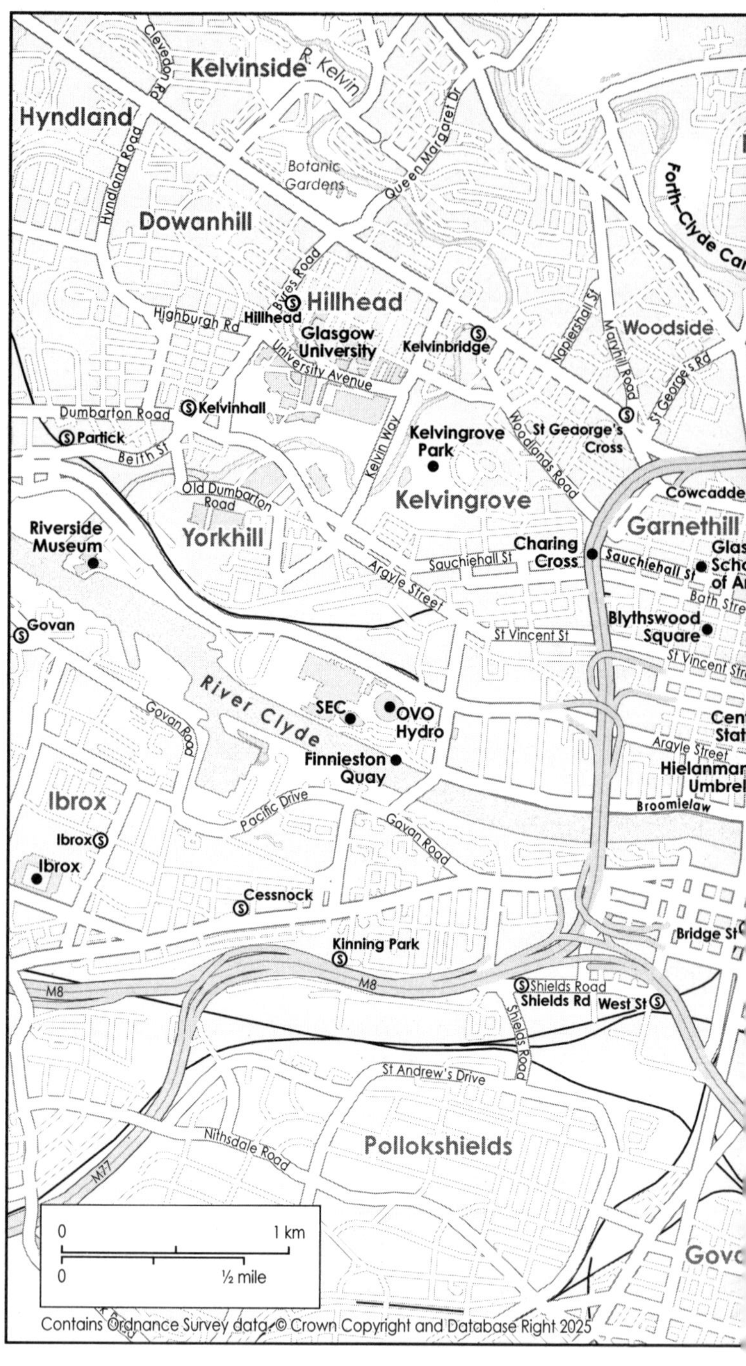

Kelvinside
Clevedon Rd
R. Kelvin
Hyndland
Hyndland Road
Botanic Gardens
Queen Margaret Dr
Dowanhill
Byres Road
Hillhead
Highburgh Rd
Hillhead
Glasgow University
Kelvinbridge
University Avenue
Napiershall St
Maryhill Road
Woodside
St George's Rd
Forth–Clyde Can
Dumbarton Road
Kelvinhall
Partick
Beith St
Kelvin Way
Kelvingrove Park
Woodlands Road
St Geaorge's Cross
Old Dumbarton Road
Kelvingrove
Cowcadde
Riverside Museum
Yorkhill
Charing Cross
Garnethill
Sauchiehall St
Sauchiehall St
Glas Scho of A
Argyle Street
Bath Stre
Govan
St Vincent St
Blythswood Square
St Vincent Str
River Clyde
Govan Road
SEC
OVO Hydro
Cent Stat
Argyle Street
Finnieston Quay
Hielanman Umbrel
Broomielaw
Ibrox
Pacific Drive
Govan Road
Ibrox
Ibrox
Cessnock
Bridge St
Kinning Park
M8
M8
Shields Road
Shields Rd
West St
Shields Road
St Andrew's Drive
Nithsdale Road
Pollokshields
M77
0
1 km
0
½ mile
Gov
Contains Ordnance Survey data © Crown Copyright and Database Right 2025

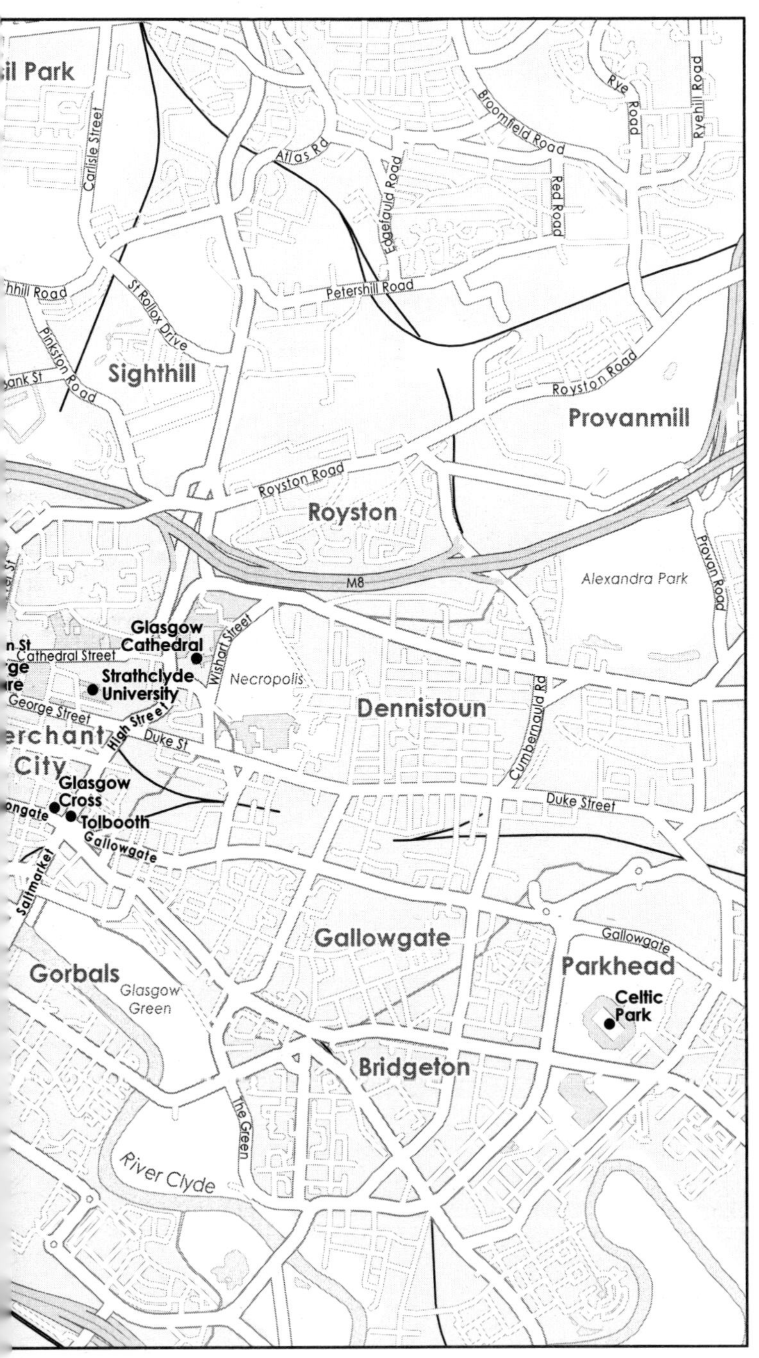

il Park
Carlisle Street
Atlas Rd
Broomfield Road
Rye Road
Ryehill Road
Edgefauld Road
Red Road
hhill Road
St Rollox Drive
Petershill Road
Pinkston Road
Sighthill
Royston Road
Provanmill
Royston Road
Royston
M8
Alexandra Park
Provan Road
Glasgow Cathedral
Wishart Street
Cathedral Street
Strathclyde University
Necropolis
George Street
High Street
Dennistoun
Cumbernauld Rd
Duke St
erchant City
Glasgow Cross
Tolbooth
Duke Street
Gallowgate
Saltmarket
Gallowgate
Gallowgate
Parkhead
Gorbals
Glasgow Green
Celtic Park
Bridgeton
The Green
River Clyde

1

The Mother City

On the afternoon of 30 June 2007, outside Terminal One at Glasgow Airport, a baggage handler was on a fly cigarette break when a Jeep Cherokee sped towards the main entrance and smashed into the security bollards. It looked like some sort of crazy ram-raid. After the two occupants emerged from the vehicle one was swiftly tackled by the police while the other presented a terrifying spectacle. The driver, Kafeel Ahmed, had doused his head and body with petrol and set himself alight. Because he had taken a great deal of morphine, the burning man felt little pain from the flames ablaze on his hair, skin and clothes. He rushed to attack the police. A taxi driver, Alex McIlveen, who had just dropped off his fare, kicked Ahmed so hard in the balls that he tore a ligament in his foot (which still hasn't healed). Another man had his leg broken in the scuffle as the terrorists fought on and attempted to get to the boot of the car to ignite the contents. The baggage handler, John Smeaton, rushed forward and kicked Ahmed hard before pulling the man with the broken leg to safety. Stephen Clarkson, who was picking up family members just back from a holiday in Benidorm, felled the burning man with a forearm smash.

It was the busiest day of the year, and there were at least 4,000 people in the terminal at that moment. All the while the Jeep was a bomb waiting to go off. The boot had been filled with containers of petrol, propane gas canisters and nails that would have acted like deadly shrapnel. Part of it appeared to be on fire. An off-duty policeman grabbed a fire extinguisher, managed to soak the car to make it safe and drenched Kaleef Ahmed. After the incident, John Smeaton was interviewed on television. Still wearing his yellow high-vis jacket, with adrenaline still surging, he was emphatic: 'They can try and come to Britain . . . you can come to Glasgow. But Glasgow disnae accept this. This is Glasgow. We'll set aboot ye. That's it.'

It was not only the instinctive courage of all the men who happened to be there at the time that ricocheted around the world's media. Smeaton's interview played from Austria to Alaska and most points between. It was also their powerful sense of themselves as citizens that resonated deeply with communities living in fear of terrorist attacks in the wake of 9/11. At that terrifying moment these men *were* Glasgow – and Glasgow disnae accept this. Representatives of a community with a distinct identity, they tackled the terrorists. That was it. The chest of every Glaswegian swelled with pride at the defiance of a taxi driver, a baggage handler, a groundsman, an off-duty policeman and several airport workers who got stuck in. But few were surprised. Their city, their people, needed at that moment to be defended, and they did not hesitate. 'I come from Glasgow' has always been more than a statement – and much, much more than an address.

Twenty years earlier Michael Marra composed a song that captured some of the reasons for all that unhesitating heroism. In 'Mother Glasgow' he sang of a maternal city that nurtures her weans, that nestles the Billy and the Tim, both Protestants and Catholics, and riffed on a dander, an imaginary walk with St Mungo, Glasgow's founder and the icon who gave the city its coat of arms and motto. A version recorded by Hue and Cry, Pat and Greg Kane, has become an informal anthem for the city.

Unlike other great cities, those perhaps more steeped, even stuck, in the past, Glasgow has no history of hesitation. It is constantly changing, moving forward. By 1980, when the A8 from Edinburgh had been upgraded to the M8, the motorway did not go around the outskirts as in other British conurbations. It pierced straight through the heart of the city like an American expressway and swept all before it.

After the Second World War, Glasgow Corporation did not hesitate to act in dealing with the housing crisis. Slum clearance in the city centre was radical as entire densely populated neighbourhoods were quickly levelled and replaced with high-rise tower blocks and peripheral housing estates. With their inside toilets, hot and cold running water and modern conveniences now taken for granted, the new council housing was generally welcomed. But it also became the butt of Glasgow's particular brand of humour. In 1967, Adam McNaughton wrote 'The Jeely Piece Song'. It mourned the passing of the three- and four-storey tenements of Govan and the Gorbals where jam sandwiches could be flung by mothers out of windows and caught by hungry weans playing in the streets and drying greens below. From the twenty-storey high-rise flats of Castlemilk, piece-flinging didn't work. Pieces went up rather than down, becoming a hazard to passing aircraft or even going into space to orbit the Earth as tiny satellites. McNaughton advocated a campaign to prevent more housing being built that was over piece-flinging height. It was a perfect example of how Glaswegians combine humour with criticism of their city and its people, criticism only they are allowed or qualified to air.

Mother Glasgow's nestling of the Billy and the Tim is only one of many paradoxes wrapped up in Glaswegian identity.

In the past two centuries, the city has become increasingly diverse and cosmopolitan with successive waves of Highland, Irish, Jewish and Asian immigration. Sharp edges and unwelcome prejudices have sometimes flared into conflict, but there has also been a growth of great cultural richness. Perhaps one of the most memorable, surprising and quirky examples is the invention of Britain's favourite national dish in Glasgow. Chicken tikka masala was created by a Bangladeshi chef in response to a diner's preferences. And emblematic of a peculiarly Glaswegian cocktail of diversity is the career of the actor and writer, Sanjeev Kohli. He was educated at St Aloysius College, a Roman Catholic school in the city centre, took a first class honours degree in mathematics at Glasgow University, played an Asian shopkeeper in the hit TV series *Still Game* (itself a cultural icon centred around the lives of Jack and Victor, two pensioners who live in a block of high-rise flats at Osprey Heights), supports the Scotland football team, wears a kilt to formal occasions and made a very successful, and very funny, advertisement for the national soft drink, Barr's Irn-Bru. Kohli had no hesitation in becoming involved with the life of the city and embracing its collective identity. His is a uniquely Glaswegian story.

For stories, true, false or imagined, are the basis of the city's sense of itself. The civic coat of arms is almost entirely mythic. Unlike the solidity of Edinburgh's mighty castle, the heraldry of Glasgow shows a mitred saint holding a crozier in one hand and conferring a blessing with the other. He is St Mungo, or Kentigern, a holy man who may have lived in the sixth or seventh century and about whom almost nothing is known for certain. Below him two salmon make an unlikely leap upwards, each with a ring in its mouth. Within the outline of a shield stands an oak tree, and perched on its top is a robin. Beside the tree is a bell, and below both another salmon. All of these are visual references to events that almost certainly never took place, miracles performed by St Mungo. Below the shield is something he might have said, and 'Let Glasgow Flourish' has become the oft-quoted motto of the city.

Glasgow is built on stories, words and ideas, some true, some false, all of them informative, and what follows is a compendium of more words, more stories, that help define the Mother City.

2

The Song of the Clyde

Beneath the high, wind-scoured moors of the Lowther Hills, where the peat hags are punctuated by stunted, gnarled thorn trees and sheep graze where they can amongst the gorse and the heather, the story of Glasgow begins.

Where Hirstane Rig and Scaw'd Law glower over a pitiless landscape, secret streams and springs search for each other. Trickling into the bowl of the plateau, they come together to form the silver thread of the Potrail Water. Out of the northern flanks of Wedder Law, the Daer Water rises and also flows north, its course shouldered and shaped by the ranges of low, pillowy hills. At the village of Watermeetings, the Potrail and the Daer become one, and the Goddess is born. She is Clutha, the mother of the Mother City, and she gave her name to the Clyde. And without the great river, without the Clyde, Glasgow would not exist and would not have flourished. Clutha's name is ancient, from the dialects of Old Welsh or Brittonic that were spoken in Scotland long before Gaelic came from Ireland or a version of English arrived from the south. In the valleys between these bleak hill ranges, amongst those who spoke Old Welsh, the tongue of the kingdom of Strathclyde, the people known as the British as late as the eleventh century, the name of Clutha, the name of the Clyde, was venerated. It means the Holy Cleanser.

At first the young river tumbles down from the high country and flows northeast before it turns to the west below Carnwath. Then it begins a long meander, circling around the woods, fields and orchards south of Lanark. In a rare moment of drama, hedged by trees, the river roars over the double-spill of the Falls of Clyde before more lazy loops between Motherwell and Hamilton. Then it is restrained, canalised, before it runs through the heart of the city to meet the sea at the Tidal Weir next to Glasgow Green. There the freshwater is held back to prevent the upstream riverbanks from drying out, crumbling or even collapsing. Below the weir was where the meander became a working river, where it was dredged and deepened, and where quays were raised and hammers ding-donged and welding sparked in the great shipyards, and where 'Clydebuilt' became a synonym for quality, strength and durability.

In 1854 the steamship *Glasgow* rounded Gourock Bay, entered the mouth of the River Clyde and ran aground near Renfrew. Its hull was badly holed by a huge rock thought at first to be a singular boulder. The Elderslie Rock turned out to be a geological dyke of hard whinstone that was 900 feet long and 300 feet wide, running under the muddy bed of the Clyde. It was blasted by underwater charges and 110,000 tons of rock removed. At that moment, the river became a great conduit, a safe and direct link between the fast-growing, vibrant city and the markets of the world beyond the Firth of Clyde.

Elsewhere, geology let Glasgow flourish. Hundreds of millions of years ago what is now the Central Belt of Scotland and Ayrshire was covered by dense tropical forests. As trees fell and the crust of the Earth convulsed and shifted, strata – seams – of coal began to form in three low-lying basins. These eventually became the coalfields of Central Scotland, Ayrshire and the Douglas Valley, what would be mined to fire Glasgow's industries from the eighteenth century onwards. More geology helped build the burgeoning city. Not only coal was laid down in the Carboniferous Period; there were also many deposits of sandstone near the surface. As Glasgow expanded, these were quarried, the stone cut and dressed, and magnificent buildings rose on the banks of the river.

Much more recently, the ice helped the city flourish. During the last Ice Age, ending only 10,000 years ago, a huge ice dome formed over Ben Lomond. Perfectly symmetrical and made smooth by the incessant hurricanes that whipped around its flanks, the ice mountain at first crushed the land underneath, and then formed it. When temperatures rose, the dome groaned and cracked and glaciers began to rumble slowly across the frozen landscape. Like giant sheets of geological sandpaper, they scarted and shaped the land on which Glasgow was to be built. North and south of the Clyde, scores of small hills known as drumlins were formed by the ice. Composed of boulder clay, bits of rock and other glacial debris, they were moulded into rounded shapes. Their location shows that the glacier flowed eastward north of the river and southeastward to the south. Modern place-names mark their location: Maryhill, Firhill, Jordanhill, Ruchill, Hillhead, Dowanhill and many others. At one time, there were no fewer than sixteen Hill Streets in Glasgow.

The city was built and grew on another set of geological consequences. It lies close to the Highland Boundary Fault that runs from Stonehaven in the North East to the southern end of Loch Lomond, no more than twenty miles from Glasgow. Beyond the Fault is another country, the Highlands, and while its proximity certainly shaped the city culturally, its nature also supplied much of the necessary raw material for expansion, especially timber and slate. To the south, east and west, and especially in the Clyde Valley, the fertile farmlands of the Lowlands would feed the growing population of the city.

The barley, oats and potatoes and lush grazing are watered by a maritime climate with moderate temperatures and frequent rain. Most days are cloudy, and sunshine is seen as a gift. When the world's most famous Glaswegian, Billy Connolly, was asked about the weather, he replied that there were only two seasons, June and winter. But despite the drizzle and the damp, the city has been blessed in all sorts of ways. For 10,000 years and long before, Clutha, the Mother Goddess has smiled on Glasgow's weans.

3

The Pioneers, the Deep World and the Wall

As well as making it, cities obliterate history. In the millennia after the ice, pioneers came north into a virgin landscape, almost certainly paddling curraghs, boats made from animal hide. The first men and women to see the Clyde after the retreat of the glaciers will have thought its banks a good place to live. Fish swam in the river and prey animals such as deer could be hunted or trapped in the wildwood of the interior. Fruits, berries, nuts and roots could be gathered, and some, like hazelnuts, roasted and ground into a nutritious paste that would keep through the hungry months of the winter. But as they flitted through the shadows under the trees, these people left only gossamer traces. At Cramond, near the shores of the Forth west of Edinburgh, the holes made by wooden rods, the framework that supported a shelter, perhaps shaped like a bender tent, were found. Near them were the remains of a hearth that could be carbon-dated to around 8,500 BC. Nothing similar has been discovered close to Glasgow.

To the northeast of the city, however, one tantalising discovery was made, a hint of the archaeological richness that almost certainly lies hidden under its streets and squares. Near Cochno Farm, north of Duntocher, not far from the A82, an outcrop of rock art was unearthed in 2016. Measuring forty-three by twenty-six feet, the biggest panel, the Cochno Stone, was described as 'the most important Neolithic art panel in Europe'. On its surface are carved a series of what are known as cup and ring marks, mysterious, swirling designs pecked out with a chisel fashioned from harder stone. Their meaning is stubbornly obscure. They may have been boundary markers, or the shallow cups and rings might have been filled with milk, mead or some other liquid, or coloured with red or yellow ochre in what could have been religious ceremonies of some unknowable sort. The Cochno Stone was first discovered in 1885 by the Reverend James Harvey, who sketched it and published his findings; in 1964 it was reburied by archaeologists to protect it from graffiti and vandalism, and then reassessed by archaeologists in 2016. It hints at a rich but now long-lost prehistoric culture in and around Glasgow.

In 150 AD, a Greek-speaking geographer known as Claudius Ptolemy made the first surviving map of Scotland. Working in Alexandria, perhaps using what remained of the famous library at the mouth of the Nile, he probably depended on military intelligence as a major source of information. Seventy years before Ptolemy began to draw an outline of the coasts of Scotland, Roman legions had invaded, attempting to extend the province of Britannia as far north as possible. As the army tramped over the Cheviot Hills and crossed the Forth, it was shadowed by the *Classis Britannica*, the Roman naval fleet based in Britain. Gnaeus Julius Agricola, the governor of the province and the commanding general, almost certainly sent ships to circumnavigate Scotland and report back on what they found. Now lost, this important record was probably the source of Ptolemy's information, especially the names of the different kindreds who controlled each region. Some appeared to bear the names of their totem animals: the Venicones of Fife were the Kindred Hounds, the Lugi of the Moray Firth, the Creones of the

Inner Hebrides and the Epidii of Kintyre were the Horse Lords. When Roman ships first sailed into the Firth of Clyde, *c.* 81 AD, their captains asked what the name of the local kindred was. Something like 'Damnonii' was the reply, the Damnonians.

Not a totem name, it is likely to be a reference to what these people did, which distinguished them from the other kindreds around the coasts of Scotland. Derived from Old Welsh, Damnonii means 'the people of the Deep World' or 'the Deepeners', 'the Diggers'. A very similar name appears elsewhere on Ptolemy's map. Devon, or Devonshire, derives from Damnonii and is probably a reference to the prehistoric tin-mining industry. Since deposits are rare in Western Europe and tin was needed to make the alloy of bronze or brass, it was much prized. Large quantities of tin ingots were smelted in Devon and exported to Europe. In the Clyde Valley and in Ayrshire, the Damnonii dug in the deep world of the coal heughs, the seams exposed on the surface. Some were very large, others narrow, and all were in danger of collapse. It has been estimated that more than a hundred major heughs in the region had been completely worked out by the early eighteenth century. The Deepeners also dug for iron ore, and there were rich, accessible deposits at Muirkirk near Cumnock, at Cambuslang and in Monklands. The close proximity of coal and iron created an industry that lasted for thousands of years, ending with the closure of Ravenscraig Steel Mills in 1992. The demolition of the familiar blue gasometer towers four years later took six seconds. Even in prehistory, the process of smelting and forging iron and steel will have been spectacular and the skills of smiths mysterious, even magical. It was an impression that endured. When Robert Burns was refused entry to the Carron Iron Works at Falkirk, because the processes were secret, he wrote:

We cam na here to view your warks,
In hopes to be mair wise,
But only, lest we gang to Hell,
It may be nae surprise.
But when we tirl'd at your door
The porter dought na bear us:
Sae may, should we to Hell's yetts come,
Your billie Satan sair us.

Only a short distance south of the site of the Cochno Stone lie the remains of another ancient monument: a frontier, the limits of ambition, a product of imperial politics, perhaps even of vanity. In 122 AD, the Roman emperor Hadrian arrived at the mouth of the Tyne to oversee the initial construction of the wall that would bear his name, the largest Roman monument in the world. Before he died in 138, this far-travelled soldier-emperor anointed Antoninus Pius as his successor. And like all successors to the imperial purple, he needed an opening blaze of prestige to establish his authority. But he did not want to leave Rome either, to abandon the city to the influence of potential conspirators. And so he wrote to the governor of Britannia, Quintus Lollius Urbicus, ordering him to march the legions north and bring southern Scotland into the empire. And to demonstrate an achievement even greater than Hadrian's, Antoninus also ordered the building of another wall – and quickly. This time it would be made from slabs of turf topped with a wooden breastwork and walkway, with a series of forts strung out along its length. Behind it ran a road, and in front a deep ditch was dug, making the rampart seem higher to any who dared to approach it.

Rising up from the eastern coastal plain at Bo'ness on the Forth shore, the line of the Antonine Wall quickly finds the high country to the south of the River Carron. Always seeking clear vistas to the north, it moves west from Croy Hill and Bar Hill before running along the southern side of the valley of the River Kelvin. At Balmuildy the line of the wall turns sharply northwest for a few hundred yards and then strikes through what is now the Glasgow suburb of Bearsden before reaching its terminus at Old Kilpatrick on the northern bank of the Clyde. Only the ford at Bowling lay beyond the end of the wall; all of the others were upstream and behind it.

Property prices in Bearsden might be thought to benefit from the presence of Roman remains. History on a doorstep adds a certain cachet. Less appealing to estate agents might be the fact that one of the most interesting and revealing finds at Bearsden's Roman fort was the effluent from a latrine. The sewage drained into the ditches beyond the rampart, where it was covered with water (and preserved in the anaerobic mud), and so probably did not smell, except perhaps on warm summer days. Analysis of the effluent has revealed a largely vegetarian diet for the average Roman soldier: oat-based cereal supplemented by wild fruits and nuts such as raspberries, brambles and hazelnuts, probably foraged in the woodland to the north and south. Nutritional habits seem to have come full circle. Two thousand years after the last soldier nipped to the loo, many breakfasts in Bearsden now contain oatmeal and fruits, berries and nuts foraged from the nearby Waitrose on Glasgow Road.

4

Mungo, Enoch and the Molendinar Burn

Rather surprisingly, suspicions of sexual misbehaviour surround the story of Mungo. He was said to have been the son of Princess Teneu, the daughter of King Lot of the Gododdin who ruled over and gave his name to the Lothians. Possibly. Legend has it that she became pregnant after being raped by the Welsh prince Owain mab Urien, who later became king of Rheged, ruling over Galloway and Cumbria. Maybe. He is one of the few actors in these tales who has a faint but genuine historical profile. As a punishment for her 'sins', somewhat unfairly, Teneu was thrown off the cliffs of Traprain Law in East Lothian, a citadel of the kings of the Gododdin. But she miraculously survived the fall and made her way, adrift in a coracle, to Culross in Fife, where she was cared for by St Serf. Very unlikely. There, sometime in the early decades of the sixth century, she gave birth to Mungo, also known as Kentigern. Teneu herself was canonised (a much more informal and local process in the early church) and her name, sometimes rendered as Tannoch, eventually meant that she was known as St Enoch. And she had a subway station named after her.

As Mungo grew up at Culross, it became clear that he was different, capable of miraculous acts like his mother, something that continued all his exemplary life. Four of his miracles are depicted in Glasgow's coat of arms, and an oft-quoted verse, which is included in Michael Marra's song, 'Mother Glasgow', goes as follows:

Here is the tree that never grew
Here is the bird that never flew
Here is the fish that never swam
Here is the bell that never rang.

The bird that sits on the tree was a pet robin cruelly killed by Mungo's classmates at the monastery at Culross and brought back to life by him. The presence of a sturdy oak tree, apart from being a handy perch for the robin, is harder to understand. Mungo had fallen asleep in front of a fire at the monastery and let it go out. To rekindle it, he went outside and found a *hazel* branch. And that's it. Not much of a miracle, not like raising the dead or, much more impressive, turning water into wine.

The three fish in the coat of arms refer to the tallest and most convoluted tale of them all. Mungo had moved from Culross close to Dumbarton Rock, known as the Rock of the Clyde and the fortress of another king with a faint historical profile. Rhydderch Hael was one of the early rulers of Alt Clut, the old kingdom of Strathclyde that lasted until the eleventh century. He was a suspicious and jealous man. Having given a ring to his queen, Languoreth, he saw it not on her finger but on that of a handsome young knight, probably her lover. As the man slept in the woods on a hunting expedition, Rhydderch slipped it off his finger and threw it in the Clyde. Later, the king asked Languoreth if he might see the ring he gave her. The punishment for such infidelity was death, and the terrified queen begged the holy man, Mungo, for help. Perhaps he remembered what had happened to his mother. In any case, Mungo sent someone to fish in the Clyde, and when they pulled out what on the coat of arms looks like a salmon, the ring was found inside the fish. All of which is clearly tosh, and also not very original. A similar story was told of King Maelgwyn of Gwynedd in Wales, in the Greek tale of Polycrates, in a Sanskrit drama and in the Talmudic tale of Solomon. The most famous variant will be familiar to many because it appears in the New Testament as the story of the tribute money. Jesus directed Peter to find a coin in the mouth of a fish so that the temple tax could be paid.

The line about the bell is also odd. It looks genuine, a reference to the sort of handbell rung by missionaries and early preachers to summon a congregation before there were churches with bell towers. So it was certainly rung. Apparently, Mungo picked it up on a visit to Rome. Not likely.

Perhaps the sole authentic item on the arms of Glasgow is the motto at the bottom. Mungo may well have said something like 'Let Glasgow flourish – by the preaching of the Word [of God]' in one of his sermons.

Later history and politics explain much about the promotion and acceptance of this unlikely mixture of mythology and miracles. In the second half of the twelfth century, Glasgow badly needed a saint, a very Scottish saint of its own.

On a reckless foray into Northumberland and a siege of Alnwick Castle, King William the Lion was captured in 1174 after an ill-advised solo charge on English troops. A year later, the Scottish king was forced by Henry II of England to agree to the terms of the Treaty of Falaise. It compelled William to become a vassal, to acknowledge the English king as his feudal superior and also to agree that the Church in Scotland should be subordinate to the Church in England and its archbishops of York and Canterbury. Recently appointed as Bishop of Glasgow, Jocelin had been Abbot of Melrose, having been a novice when the great monastery had been in the care of the charismatic Waltheof of Northampton. He was believed by many to have been a saintly man, but in 1159 the Pope in Rome had claimed the exclusive right of canonisation. Since the days of Columba, Aidan and Cuthbert, sainthood had been a matter of local acclamation often reinforced by a vita, a life of the holy man that listed the necessary conditions for canonisation, including a series of miracles. As Abbot of Melrose, Jocelin commissioned the hagiographer Jocelyn of Furness to write a vita of Waltheof, and it had the desired effect.

When the Treaty of Falaise specified that the Bishop of Glasgow was to become the subordinate of the Archbishop of York, Jocelin had to move quickly, and he immediately contacted his namesake of Furness. Allegedly using an ancient Gaelic manuscript as source material (for a story told in Old Welsh?) and other bits and bobs that came to hand, Jocelyn rapidly knocked up a vita of St Mungo. It is also the source of almost all the tall tales of Teneu and the miracles on Glasgow's coat of arms. But more importantly, it worked, conferring high status on the cathedral. It became the centre of the cult of St Mungo, a very Scottish saint who made the church distinct, different from York and England, and it also made the bishopric much more wealthy.

Pilgrimage to the shrines of saints was lucrative as offerings were left and often payment made for masses to be said for the dead, the sick and the living. It was seen as vital for the pilgrims to come to the shrine in person, to the cathedral, for what mattered was propinquity. If penitents could get close to the relics, the bones and possessions of the saints, as close as possible, it was much more likely that through their intercession God would hear and heed their prayers. The remains of the old shrine of Mungo are in the cathedral crypt and they reveal how those pilgrims prayed. Shaped like a miniature church, the reliquary containing the saint's remains sat on arches made by twelve pillars. These were spaced sufficiently widely to allow penitents to put their heads between them to pray and even, in some cases, position themselves more directly beneath the reliquary so that their voices could ascend through Mungo's holy bones up to Heaven.

Bishop Jocelin also played papal politics very adroitly. He petitioned the Church of Rome for special recognition for his see of Glasgow and, when challenged by the Archbishop of York, was able to quote from a papal bull. It asserted that Glasgow was 'a special daughter' of the papacy, a relationship that went over the head of the English archbishop.

Mungo himself was probably no stranger to playing politics, and may indeed have seen himself as a minor aristocrat, the son of a princess. His alternative name is Kentigern, and the last element is cognate to the Old Welsh and Gaelic root words Tigernos and Tighearna, both of which mean 'lord'. Mungo is a diminutive 'dear one'. Culross, where he was said to have been born, was probably not a monastery in the medieval sense that Melrose was. In the sixth century, monks tended to be hermits, solitaries, the literal meaning of the former coming from the Greek *monachos*, to be alone. Sometimes they lived in small communities with separate cells, where they could pray, fast, meditate and try to communicate directly with God. Repetition was important, and the solitaries invented the prayer rope or rosary to count the number offered up to God. These communities were known as 'diseartan', a memory of the original solitaries like St Anthony of Egypt, who lived in the deserts, apart from the temporal world. Further along the Fife coast is Dysart, where there certainly was another diseart.

When Mungo came to the banks of the Clyde and to the kingdom of Strathclyde of Rhydderch Hael, he did not seek to found a diseart near his fortress at Dumbarton Rock. That was emphatically part of the temporal world. Instead, he built a cell and perhaps a small wooden chapel on the banks of the Molendinar Burn, a small tributary of the Clyde, a safe distance from the king and his roistering warriors. When he came to found the community on Lindisfarne a few decades later, St Aidan was similarly prudent. Not wishing to be close to the Northumbrian kings in their fortress on Bamburgh's rock, but close enough, he chose the tidal island a few miles to the north. Mungo's choice of the Molendinar Burn is the reason why Glasgow's cathedral is where it is.

5

The Rock of the Clyde

No matter how colourful his miracles, and no matter how much Bishop Jocelin inflated his reputation. St Mungo was not the Apostle of Strathclyde. When he arrived in the later sixth century, the kingdom was already Christian. Sometime in the late fifth century, St Patrick wrote a letter to the soldiers of Coroticus, the king of Alt Clut. It opens memorably with: 'I declare that I, Patrick, – an unlearned sinner indeed – have been established a bishop in Ireland. I hold quite certainly that what I am, I have accepted from God. I live as an alien among non-Roman peoples, an exile on account of the love of God – he is my witness that this is so.'

In the letter, the saint complains that the warband of Strathclyde has been raiding in Ireland, killing fellow Christians and carrying off more into slavery. It is a rare piece of contemporary documentary evidence for the period commonly known as the Dark Ages, and it is illuminating about the culture of the kingdom of the Clyde.

Despite his close, even defining association, Patrick was not Irish. He was probably born and raised in an early Christian community located in and around Carlisle. He himself had been captured by slavers and sold in Ireland where he worked as a shepherd boy before escaping. Patricius probably knew a good deal about Strathclyde and its kings. Coroticus appears to have lived in a post-Roman cultural milieu where a letter written in Latin to 'fellow citizens' was understood. Christianity was seen as the religion of Rome, the empire's most important and lasting legacy. By the end of the sixth century, the Old Welsh-speaking kingdoms of *Yr Hen Ogledd*, the Old North, were calling themselves *Y Bedydd*, the Baptised. Those who were not yet Christians – the Picts in the north and the Angles to the south – were *Y Gynt*, the Gentiles, the Heathens.

Such was the political and cultural atmosphere in Strathclyde when Mungo arrived, perhaps in the 570s, to found his community by the Clyde and the Molendinar Burn. It was probably a diseart, bounded by water, the river and the stream, and thereby set apart from the temporal world. Similar diseartan were established in the confluences of rivers, the Tweed at Old Melrose in the Borders being the best known and most prestigious. Even if he was not a pioneering missionary, Mungo was nonetheless venerated in his lifetime. One of the few authentic notes in the stories that swirled around him speaks of a man who lived to a great age for the times. Apparently Mungo's jaw became so slack that the brothers bound it up with a cloth when he appeared in public, perhaps to stop the old man from drooling. It may be that he finally collapsed, at the age of eighty or thereabouts, during a baptismal service in 612.

Rhydderch Hael, the king who welcomed and supported Mungo as well as testing his miraculous powers, was the descendant of Coroticus, and his title marked him as 'a gold-giver'. Hael means generous in Old Welsh. He rewarded his warband, the warriors who attended him at Alt Clut, from the proceeds of looting and raiding. These men will have policed the realm of Strathclyde, for, unusually, it was bounded by clear borders that are still remembered in the secret language of place-names.

Once the A82 has wiggled around the western shores of Loch Lomond, it enters Glen Falloch. Close to the road is a striking, spectacular hunk of geology, a huge boulder commanding the wide moorland, looking as though the mighty hand of God had placed it carefully on a rocky knoll. In fact it marks an ancient frontier, the northern border of the old kingdom of Strathclyde. It is the Clach nam Breatann, the Stone of the Britons, the Old Welsh speakers of Alt Clut. It also marks the place where three kingdoms once met: the Gaelic-speakers of Dalriada in the west and the Picts in the north. Such long-lasting precision was unusual, for kingdoms were more often networks of loyalty and obligation in the Dark Ages rather than territory marked by physical boundaries.

Place-names trace the line of the frontier as it runs south-west to Cnap na Criche, the Hill of the Border, before reaching the head of Loch Goil where another version of the Stone of the British, the Clach nam Breatann, stands sentinel. Identifiable by a long string of *crìochan*, frontier names, the border between Strathclyde and Dalriada reaches Blairlomond, the Field of the Beacon, which was lit when raiders sailed up the Firth of Clyde or rode over the high mountain passes. On the eastern shore of the great loch, Ben Lomond means Beacon Mountain and its flanks were used for the same purpose. In the Firth of Clyde, there were coastal forts on Bute and the Cumbraes, an old name that means the Isles of the Britons. To the east, Strathclyde's land border extended almost to Tyndrum and a clearly identifiable quartzite ridge called Druim Alban, the Ridge of Britain.

Meanwhile, the venerable Mungo appears to have established a community distinct from the royal fortress at Alt Clut, although no doubt enjoying the protection of Rhydderch Hael the generous. In Old Welsh, these early monasteries were known as *clasau*, and several still survive in place-names in Wales. It translates as 'family', and with the addition of *gu*, the term supplies the most likely derivation for the subsequent name of the city that would eventually grow up around the site. *Clas-gu* means 'dear family'. If Clutha was the Mother of the Mother City, then surely Mungo was the Father of Glasgow, the City of the Dear Family.

To the north of the *clas* at Alt Clut, half-forgotten Strathclyde kings like Beli and Teudebur raided and defended, all the while doggedly maintaining the independence of their kingdom and its borders. It was not until 870 that the Rock of the Clyde was assailed and its citadel breached. That summer, sentries on the high ramparts shouted for their captains to come and behold a belly-hollowing sight. Sailing around Gourock Bay and into the mouth of the river were 200 Viking longships, and standing in two of the prows were the kings of Dublin, Olaf and Ivar. After a four-month siege, the garrison of Alt Clut was forced to surrender. Their well had dried up. Instead of suffering great slaughter, they and the nobility of Strathclyde were made captive and carried off to be sold at the great slave market in Dublin. Supposedly at the request of the Pictish king, Causantín mac Cináeda (anglicised to King Constantine I of Alba), King Artgal of Alt Clut was put to death by his Viking captors.

Somehow, and the sources are scant and obscure, the kingdom of Strathclyde survived. At Govan Old Parish Church there are fascinating fragments of sculpture (that should be better known) that suggest renewal. Cross-slabs and shafts and a sarcophagus may be relics of a sacred precinct and a new royal centre for the old kingdom. There is also a series of impressive Viking hogback tombs that speak of a more cosmopolitan culture. They may house the bones of merchants.

In the tenth century, kings probably based at Govan were negotiating with Athelstan of Wessex as his armies marched north to subjugate England and invade Scotland. In 936, as the king and governor of all Britain, Athelstan received the submission of Owain of Strathclyde. It seemed that Owain's kingdom had expanded far to the south to take in Galloway and Cumbria. There is a tenacious popular local tradition in the Lake District of a Cumbrian king, Dunmail, fighting a battle on the pass between Thirlmere and Grasmere, and, surprisingly, a retail park near Workington is named after him. Dunmail was almost certainly Dyfnwal, King of Strathclyde.

At Caddonlea, a wide and level area of haughland near the Tweed, close to Galashiels, a great army mustered a thousand years ago. King Malcolm II of Alba was making war against the Earls of Bamburgh, the rulers of old Northumbria, for control of the rich farmland of the Borders. And from the west, the host of King Owain of Strathclyde had come to join him. In 1018, at the hamlet of Carham, on the banks of the Tweed, the English spearmen were cut to pieces and the line of the modern border between England and Scotland was more or less fixed. It was an important moment in Scotland's history for that reason, and also for another. King Owain was probably killed in the ruck of the hand-to-hand fighting, and when he fell, so did his ancient kingdom. No more was heard of the old realm of Strathclyde.

6

The King-Bishops

The kingdom of Strathclyde did not disappear with the death of Owain at Carham; it assumed another name. When King Malcolm Canmore died in 1093, his son, David, could never have expected to become his heir. The youngest of six sons, he could look forward to a privileged life as a nobleman, or perhaps take holy orders and become a prince of the church. But when his brothers began to pre-decease him, rapidly, that sort of comfortable future evaporated.

After the death of his father and the subsequent jostling for power at court, the boy David was taken south by his sister, Maud, for his own, and also her, protection. The MacMalcolms were a ruthless dynasty, unhesitating in pursuit of personal ambition, unhesitating in the removal of rivals.

As the fourth son of William the Conqueror, Henry's expectations were also limited. As with David, fate played out differently, and he eventually succeeded to the throne of England as Henry I in 1100. And crucially, he married Maud, David's sister. The young man's status as 'brother of the queen' gained him estates in England and probably something of an education in France. David visited Tiron Abbey in Perche, south of Normandy, and was much impressed by how the monks, far from withdrawing from worldly affairs, had stimulated the local economy by organising land-holding and management, maximising yields and bringing virgin ground into cultivation.

And, most importantly, David met a monk who became his chaplain, John Capellanus, a man whose influence on the young man – and on early Glasgow – would be profound.

At his Christmas court at Winchester in 1113, Henry I gave David a great gift. He offered Matilda, an extremely wealthy and widely landed widow, to David in marriage so that Henry could have a loyal and dependable subject in the north should trouble ever threaten to cross the border. The English king also put pressure on Alexander I of Scotland to make his younger brother, now his heir, *Princeps Cumbrensis*. David became Prince of Cumbria, an alternative name for the old kingdom of Strathclyde. His lands included the Clyde Valley, Teviotdale and much of Tweeddale. Also in 1113, he and John Capellanus persuaded the Abbot of Tiron to send thirteen monks to found a daughter house, a new monastery that eventually settled at Kelso, where the building of the great abbey began in 1128.

In 1124 David was the first of that name to become king of Scotland. That the traditional royal names of Malcolm, Duncan and Kenneth from a Gaelic-speaking past were succeeded by the biblical name of David was more than symbolic. The new king remade and modernised Scotland with the help of John Capellanus. Sometime before the consecration of the cathedral in 1136, David had appointed his chaplain as Bishop of Glasgow. Indeed, it may have been John who had set in train the construction of the new church in 1119. His diocese was vast. From the old frontier at Glen Falloch in the north, it comprised the whole of the Clyde Valley: what is now Ayrshire, Dumfriesshire and almost all of the Teviot and Tweed Valleys. It was by far the largest, richest, most fertile diocese in Scotland, it made Capellanus enormously powerful, and it brought the old kingdom of Strathclyde back to life, if in heavy disguise.

When John died in 1147, David I sent for Herbert from the Tironensian abbey at Kelso to succeed him and carry on the work of modernisation – and supply continuity. When Malcolm IV succeeded to David's throne in 1153, he was only twelve years old and needed support from a loyal nobility. Ten years later, his rule still shaky, another king in Scotland challenged Malcolm. Styled as Ri Innse Gall, 'the king of the islands of the strangers' (the name given to the Hebrides after settlement by the Vikings), and also known as the Lord of the Isles, Somerled mustered a huge fleet and sailed up the Clyde and into the heart of the kingdom.

Medieval bishops often did not hesitate to buckle on their chain mail with a sword belt, and Herbert led a force to meet the Islesmen when they landed at Renfrew. And they were lucky. In what seems like a chance encounter, perhaps a preliminary skirmish, Somerled himself was felled 'by a [thrown] spear and cut down by the sword'. At the loss of their charismatic leader, the Islesmen scrambled aboard their birlinns and sailed away. A priest hacked off the Hebridean king's head as a trophy, and it was said that a triumphant Herbert displayed it in his cathedral.

Bishop Jocelin's skills were more diplomatic than martial. But like the Tironensians, he was anxious to see the economy develop. A close confidant to King William the Lion, he persuaded him to grant the bishop's town of Glasgow burgh status in 1175. This was important because it enabled a weekly market to be held, making it a focal point for local food producers. Rutherglen had become a royal burgh in 1128, but it lay on the other side of the Clyde, and Lanark was some distance away to the southeast. A weekly market brought not only activity but also revenue from tolls, taxes and fines paid by stallholders and buyers, and it began the slow expansion of the town.

Glasgow's new status brought new people with specialist skills. As Abbot of Melrose, Jocelin will have been familiar with the organisation and layout of Roxburgh, another, much larger royal burgh founded by David I near his abbey at Kelso. The bishop brought in a man called Ranulf of Haddington to supervise. Once the location of the weekly market had been established at Glasgow Cross, the setting out of house plots had to ensure that there was enough space for stalls to be set up in the wide street, for animals to be penned and for buyers and sellers to move around. Access to the burgh needed to be controlled and gates set up. Town walls were expensive, and new burghs were often encircled by ditches and an earthen bank formed from the upcast. What was known as 'quickset' (fast-growing thorn bushes, the long and sharp needles of blackthorn especially effective) was planted in the ditch to discourage uncontrolled entrance and exit for those who sought to avoid paying tolls. Inside the town boundary, liners measured out long and narrow house-plots. Most had their gable-ends facing the street and behind them were long back-lands where produce could be grown, a milk cow tethered, and waste, of all sorts, disposed of. In some old Scottish towns, like St Andrews, these long backlands have been preserved.

By the early thirteenth century the line of the High Street was well established, and evidence suggests that it had become extensively built up by 1285. More development formed the hub of the medieval town around the Saltmarket, the Trongate, the Gallowgate and the High Street. 'Gate' or 'gait' is a Norse-derived Scots word for a street. The Trongate was where tolls were collected and standardised weighing operated, and the Gallowgate was occasionally the place where gallows were set up and hushed crowds formed to watch an execution. The focus of much activity and most of the market stalls was around Glasgow Cross. All of these new buildings and streets rose up on the higher ground, above the flood plain of the Clyde. And at some point a wooden bridge was built across the river at the foot of what became the Briggait Port.

In 1190 Bishop Jocelin added to the gaiety of Glasgow when he persuaded William the Lion to grant permission to hold the first fair in late July. It may have lasted several days and taken place in the cathedral precinct. A market was certainly set up, no doubt foodstuffs and drinks were sold, and a great deal of enjoyment was had. Games like hurling or early versions of hand ba', an ancestor of rugby, may have been played. And music was likely to have been part of the fun of the fair. Over time the festival evolved into Fair Fortnight when almost every business in Glasgow closed, both factories and offices. Fair Monday remains a public holiday in the middle of July.

7

The Two Roberts

In the black darkness of a stormy late winter's night in March 1286, King Alexander rode along the clifftop path at Pettycur on the Forth shore of Fife. Fuelled by wine and ardour, it was later said, he was determined to visit his new bride, Yolande de Dreux, at his royal manor at Kinghorn. Perhaps the wind suddenly gusted, and the horse spooked. What is certain is that Alexander plunged over the cliff edge to his death. It was a turning moment, the beginning of the end of the great MacMalcolm dynasty and the beginning of a long period of instability that began with the Wars of Independence.

Six Guardians of the Realm were appointed to govern the kingless kingdom, and when it became clear that a successor to Alexander had to be chosen, Edward I of England demanded to meet them.

In the summer of 1291, in the great hall of Norham Castle, in the presence of the king enthroned and surrounded by his great barons, Roger Brabazon, an English justice, told the Scots something they had not expected to hear. Edward I would not be a friendly arbiter but a supreme judge – as was his right as the overlord of Scotland, something that had been agreed a hundred years before in the Treaty of Falaise. And more than that, it seems that the king had encouraged many other competitors to present themselves for consideration. Instead of two, Robert Bruce and John Balliol, there would now be twelve, almost all of them English noblemen descended from the illegitimate offspring of Scottish kings, of whom there appeared to be many. It was a genealogical maze, and probably a device to cloud the issue and make firm judgement all the more desirable.

Much winded by Edward's bullish and uncompromising approach, the Scots protested. One of the Guardians of the Realm was Robert Wishart, Bishop of Glasgow, and he seems to have been quick-thinking and eloquent, as well as courageous. The king had summoned many of his barons to the parliament at Norham, and no doubt they rode north at the head of armed retinues. It was a show of England's great strength. Six hundred and fifty crossbowmen had also arrived to bolster the castle garrison, and anchored off Lindisfarne was an English war fleet. There was an unmistakable sense that, if diplomacy failed, the English king would not hesitate to use force.

Nevertheless, Wishart spoke up and spoke well. Edward's demand to be recognised as overlord was something that could be conceded only by a king, and the Scots delegates were in no position to do that in the absence of a legitimate king. In addition, the bishop argued that it was not incumbent on the Scots to disprove the English king's claims but that he should prove them lawful. Edward was almost certainly not accustomed to being spoken to in such a frank and direct manner and be contradicted so directly in public, and when Wishart made his final point, the king grew very angry. As a prince, Edward had gone on crusade to the Holy Land, and as someone who had sworn the vows of a crusader, said the bold bishop, the king should not be threatening a defenceless people like the Scots with war. Edward exploded. He was indeed a crusader, the king roared, and he would lead a new crusade against the Scots.

Known as the Warrior-Bishop, Robert Wishart had been consecrated in 1272 or 1273 and held the great see of Glasgow until his death in 1316. For all of those forty-odd years, he was a tireless fighter for the cause of Scottish independence, and with James Stewart, High Steward of Scotland, he raised an army, led a rising and encouraged William Wallace to take up arms. Timber allocated for the repair of his cathedral was used to build siege engines, and observers wrote of him as 'a man of war', not a man of God. Forced to surrender at Irvine in July 1297, Wishart was imprisoned for two years before, no doubt with his fingers crossed behind his back, swearing fealty to Edward I. But he continued to plot and to support Wallace. In 1301 Edward I wrote to Pope Boniface VIII demanding Wishart's removal from Glasgow. Boniface refused, but in scolding his bishop made an accurate historical assessment. He was 'the prime mover and instigator of all the tumult and dissension which has arisen between his dearest son in Christ, Edward, King of England, and the Scots'. Indeed he was.

In common with other Scottish bishops, Robert Wishart saw Scottish independence as indivisible from the independence of the Scottish Church, but unlike the diplomat Bishop Jocelin he had to fight for it all his long life. On 10 February 1306 Robert Bruce and his companions killed John Comyn III of Badenoch, one of his most serious rivals for the crown, in the chapel of the Franciscan monastery in Dumfries. It was a gross act of sacrilege that should have brought an automatic sentence of excommunication from Holy Mother Church and the certainty of eternal damnation. And the murder had taken place in a church in the diocese of Glasgow. But when Robert Bruce rode immediately to Glasgow to see Wishart, instead of censure he received absolution.

At that moment, speed was essential, and what seems like a pre-ordained plan went into action. Wishart and Bruce went to Scone, the traditional site of Scottish coronations, and where the Stone of Destiny had waited for new kings to sit on it. But in 1296 Edward I had removed the stone and all of the Scottish regalia, including the crown. Nevertheless, they met with the bishops of St Andrews and Moray as well as many noblemen and their retinues. With Bruce wearing robes borrowed from Robert Wishart, the new king was crowned with a simple circlet of gold.

Soon after the ceremony, the new king's army was scattered at the Battle of Methven, near Perth. Bishop Wishart was captured at Cupar in Fife and, by that time an old man, taken south in chains. He was only spared the grisly sentence of being hung, drawn and quartered for treason because of his status as a priest. For eight long years, the Warrior-Bishop was imprisoned in the dungeons of English castles where he gradually went blind. Robert was released as part of a prisoner exchange after the battle at Bannockburn in 1314.

As Pope Boniface wrote at the time, and as modern historians have since confirmed, the continuing independence of Scotland owed a great deal to the courage and constancy of Robert Wishart, Bishop of Glasgow.

8

Glasgow and the Godly Commonwealth

On a cold, late March morning in 1539, soldiers in the service of the Archbishop of Glasgow were busy. Probably in the open ground to the west of the cathedral, they dug two deep holes and rammed and chocked into them long, thick poles of unseasoned wood. A large crowd had begun to gather as the soldiers laid large bundles of kindling and larger logs around the base of the two stakes before smearing everything with tar.

Once all had been made ready, the archbishop's men formed a wide cordon around the pyres they had built. As the cathedral bells tolled, the west doors swung open and a short procession emerged, led by a black-clad priest and more soldiers. They escorted two captives, bound at their wrists and shivering in linen sarks. The crowd may have jeered, but given the temper of the times and recent events that had taken place in Edinburgh, that seems unlikely. Most will have watched in silence. Perhaps some bowed their heads.

Jerome Russell was a Franciscan friar, and it may be that when he saw the stakes, he held his head high, defiant to the last. Beside him walked Alexander Kennedy. Only eighteen years old, he may not have been so self-possessed in the face of the fate that awaited them both. It had been thirty years and more since Martin Luther had ignited another fire, one that blazed across Europe as the demand for the reformation of the Catholic Church gathered momentum. But in Scotland King James V and his French Queen, Mary of Guise, had remained resolutely Catholic, and Cardinal David Beaton, Primate of the Scottish Church, was determined to keep the tide of reform at bay by making examples of those who dared to question the doctrine and authority of Holy Mother Church. On 28 February, only weeks before the trial of Russell and Kennedy for heresy in the cathedral chapter house, five men had been burned at the stake on Castle Hill in Edinburgh.

When the small procession reached the stakes set up outside Glasgow Cathedral, it paused. Both of the condemned men were permitted to fall to their knees and offer up prayers for the salvation of their souls. And then, it was later reported, Russell turned to the young Kennedy and said: 'Brother, fear not: more potent is He that is in us, than He that is in the world; the pain we shall suffer is short, and shall be light, but our joy and consolation shall never have an end.'

The pain of the hideous ordeal they were about to undergo would indeed be great, but it may not have been short. For both men had been sentenced to be burned alive. Executioners were sometimes allowed to strangle the condemned before their pyres were lit. But that did not happen, and Russell and Kennedy suffered appalling agonies once the archbishop's soldiers had plunged their pitch-soaked torches into the bundles of kindling at their feet. As the flames crackled, it could be a mercy if there was no wind and the men were quickly asphyxiated by the wood smoke. But ten years before, in St Andrews, when Patrick Hamilton was burned at the stake outside St Salvator's Chapel, a wind blew off the North Sea and he took six hours to die.

These acts of barbaric cruelty were a prelude to seismic change in Scotland. The Catholic Church had been maintained after her husband's death in 1542 by the support of Queen Mary of Guise and contingents of French soldiers. But when she died in 1560 and her soldiers boarded ships at Leith, an unstoppable tide of reform was undammed. A parliament was convened in Edinburgh, and led by John Knox, a committee drew up the Confession of Faith, an extraordinarily comprehensive manifesto for the creation of a Protestant Church of Scotland. There was some rioting and some destruction – Scone Abbey was reduced to rubble and much sculpture and stained glass was smashed – but the transition was relatively smooth. Surprisingly, after the treatment of Russell and Kennedy, Glasgow Cathedral survived virtually intact. And so did one of its more humane and productive cultural initiatives.

Glasgow University was founded in 1451 when Bishop William Turnbull persuaded the Pope to issue a bull enabling its creation, making it the second oldest in Scotland and the fourth oldest in the English-speaking world. Devoted in its early years to the teaching of theology and the training of priests, the university held its first classes in the chapterhouse of the cathedral. Perhaps because there was a demand for places, students were then taught in a larger building called the Auld Pedagogy. How suitable and salubrious it was may be a matter for conjecture for it stood in Rottenrow, or Rat Row, so called since its buildings were notoriously infested. Mary, Queen of Scots and the Reformation came to the rescue in 1563 when she gave the university thirteen acres of land in the High Street that had belonged to the Dominican order, disbanded only a few years earlier. Perhaps Jerome Russell looked down and smiled as students filed into lectures.

In 1574, a truly remarkable man, one of the greatest to grace public life in Scotland, was appointed Principal of the University of Glasgow. Andrew Melville was both an educational and ecclesiastical reformer resolute in his beliefs and ready to die for them. He immediately enlarged the university's curriculum, establishing the teaching of modern languages as well as Latin and Greek, and also the sciences and philosophy. Such was his reputation that students came to study at Glasgow from all over Scotland, from England and from Europe.

More important, Melville had a motive hand in effecting a radical cultural change across the whole of Scottish society. The constitution of the new Church of Scotland, known as *The First Book of Discipline* (its sixteenth-century meaning being cognate to the sense of being a disciple rather than the more modern gloss) had been drawn up in 1560 by a committee that included John Knox. In 1578 Andrew Melville became Moderator of the General Assembly and he vigorously promoted and updated an expanded version, *The Second Book of Discipline*. It enshrined the central principle of the priesthood of all believers and the creation of a Godly Commonwealth in Scotland, central tenets of the Scottish Reformation.

In the Catholic Church, the faithful could only communicate with God through the intercession of priests. Even the sacrament of holy communion was hidden from the view of worshippers behind a rood screen, and the services were in any case unintelligible to most since they were conducted in Latin. The reformers changed all of this radically. All those who believed in the Lord Jesus Christ would become responsible for their own salvation, and to achieve this, every man – and woman – had to be able to read the Word of God for themselves, thereby becoming the priesthood of all believers. That in turn required a programme of mass literacy, a school in every parish and a college in every town to teach the teachers.

Because the reformed church had been immediately impoverished as secular lords grabbed most of the lands and properties of the old abbeys and churches in the years after 1560, this took more than a century and a half to achieve. But the eventual consequence of this doctrine was that Scotland became the first nation where most of its people could read, write and count. Andrew Melville, Glasgow University and the other Scottish universities were at the heart of this extraordinary cultural revolution.

Like Bishop Robert Wishart, Melville was famously outspoken in the company of kings. Sometime after 1590, he found himself at Falkland Palace in Fife in a private audience with James VI. Melville's nephew, James, was in attendance and he recorded what his uncle said. Taking the king by the sleeve and pointing out that he was 'God's sillie vassal' ('sillie' meaning humble in the sixteenth century), he explained the nature of the monumental changes that had overtaken his realm:

> Sir, we will humblie reverence your Majestie always, namlie in public, but sen we have this occasioun to be with your Majestie in privat . . . And thairfor Sir, as divers times befor, sa now again, I mon tell yow, there is twa Kings and twa Kingdomes in Scotland. Thair is Chryst Jesus the King, and his Kingdome the Kirk, whase subject King James the Saxt is, and of whose kingdome nocht a king, nor a lord, nor a heid, bot a member!

Not only is this part of a rare, authentic, contemporary record, it is also an echo of Melville's own voice and dialect, how people spoke the Scots of 1590, both the churchman and the king, a common language. One that could sometimes be blunt.

9

Glasgow and the Union

With the death of Elizabeth I of England in 1603, her heir, James VI, now I, could not get out of Scotland fast enough to escape the rantings of Andrew Melville. No one from the Church of England, of which he was definitely, legally, the Head and not a common member, would dare to talk to him like that. The Union of the Crowns meant that Edinburgh lost the royal court and all of its associated prestige and patronage. A century later, the parliaments were united, and while the capital saw a further and profound loss in status, Glasgow suddenly gained an empire.

The people of Glasgow may have rioted and demonstrated against the Treaty of Union with England, but if the Union had not happened, Glasgow would not have been the industrial powerhouse it became in the nineteenth century – the Second City of the Empire. Until 1707 it was illegal for Scots traders of any persuasion to trade with England's colonies. Anybody who did – and some did – was taking a serious risk.

The Union of 1707 changed that. From then on it was perfectly legal for Scots traders to become involved in the business of tobacco grown in Virginia or North Carolina (or sugar grown in the Caribbean islands). And the Glasgow merchants enjoyed a great commercial advantage. Their ships could be out into the open Atlantic long before ships from London, Bristol or Liverpool navigated their way up or around the coast of Ireland. Glasgow's geography cut days (and sometimes weeks) off transatlantic crossings. It was a simple effect of the curvature of the Earth. The further north a transatlantic voyage, the shorter it is. The Trade Winds also had an impact since all eighteenth-century shipping was under sail. Just as in the case of modern air travel from the Americas to Britain, the return journey for the merchant ships was considerably faster as sails billowed with the prevailing northeasterlies.

And where English merchants often acted as 'agents' for the tobacco growers, selling their product in Europe and taking a commission for doing it, the Glasgow merchants bought the goods on the spot or traded them for manufactured goods brought from Europe. Which, of course, gave the smaller tobacco growers in particular the money to buy what they needed to develop their plantations. The system worked well enough although many growers complained that they were being fleeced and that the Scots paid too little. Of course they did.

Tobacco meant Atlantic crossings, and that meant ships. And the cheapest ships that could be found were built in America and a few on the lower Clyde. Most of them cost around £500, wood-built schooners mainly, sturdy enough but usually with sufficient sail to make one crossing (there and back) each year. But many of the Glasgow-run ships, with their geographic advantage and the Trade Winds behind them, managed two crossings. The names of these little (by modern standards) ships became well known around the Clyde: *Albion*, *Katie*, *Cunninghame*, *Endeavour*, *Jupiter* and *Charming Fanny*.

The tobacco merchants did what they could to keep the trade alive all through the American War of Independence. Not only did they have the hostility of the America growers to contend with: the Atlantic and the Caribbean were swarming with French and American privateers intent on capturing or destroying British merchant ships. No one seems sure how many tobacco ships went to the bottom between 1776 and 1783, but the figure is probably more than 100. The most dangerous stretches of water seem to have been the Irish Sea and the Scottish west coast, areas the Royal Navy found it hard to police. In the end, the merchants who became known as the Tobacco Lords tried to defend themselves by arming their ships with expensive Carron-built 'carronades' from the Falkirk foundry Robert Burns was not allowed to see.

The 1770s were the peak of the Glasgow/American tobacco trade. In 1771 a total of 47,268,873 pounds of tobacco were landed at Scottish ports. A vast quantity – and very valuable. Four years later, it was down slightly to 45,863,154. These were the kind of figures that stretched to bursting the warehouses at Port Glasgow and Greenock. But those were the golden days. By 1778, after two years of warfare in America, the market crashed as the import of tobacco shrank drastically.

But Glasgow survived – and thrived. The amount of tobacco being unloaded on the Clyde piers shrank drastically, compared to what it used to be, but that was misleading. Many of the merchants had taken to shipping their goods directly to France (always the biggest customer) or landing their tobacco in English ports like Liverpool, Bristol and London.

And as Glasgow had had the benefits of the tobacco trade for almost seventy-five years, many of its vast profits had been invested in other local industries. Shipbuilding, textiles, tanneries, canals, chemical plants all benefited from tobacco money in one way or another. In fact many of the Tobacco Lords had long been influential partners in firms, in other trades.

They were men of great wealth. And they knew how to flaunt it. These merchants were famous for strutting around the streets with gold-topped canes and the fanciest of clothes. They built big houses in the city and large estates in the countryside. Some gave their names to the streets of the city – the likes of Glassford, Ingram, Gordon and Buchanan.

But there was a very dark side to all of this brisk and highly profitable enterprise, a huge price paid in human lives and unimaginable misery. The notorious Triangular Trade saw cargoes of manufactured goods taken down the western coasts of Africa where they were exchanged for slaves. These captives, often cruelly shackled, were crammed into ships that sailed across the Atlantic to the Americas and the Caribbean islands. As many as one in ten died on the voyage known as the Middle Passage. On arrival, the slaves were often taken to 'proving camps' where they were beaten into submission before being sold to plantation owners and ruthlessly worked and exploited. The tobacco, sugar, cotton and other products were then transported back to Britain and Europe.

Compared to Liverpool, Bristol and other British ports, very few slave ships sailed from Glasgow; nevertheless the city's merchants were deeply complicit in the Triangular Trade and many Scots were involved directly. Without slave labour on the plantations, such vast profits would not have been possible and investments in other industries may not have happened. There can be no doubt that the infamies of the slave trade helped Glasgow flourish.

10

The Glasgow Enlightenment

There are not many cities that can claim their own version of Victor Frankenstein, but Glasgow can. His name was Andrew Ure and he was Professor of Natural Philosophy at the Andersonian Institute (now the University of Strathclyde). One of its buildings is named after him – which is surprising since he was one of the most unpopular men in early nineteenth-century Glasgow: cantankerous, grasping, excessively hard-headed and hostile. Karl Marx knew Ure and described him as 'an enemy to society'.

Nevertheless, he had a brilliant, visionary mind and could see that electricity was about to change the world. Ure was particularly interested in the effects of electricity on the human body – what was called 'galvanisation' – something that was the subject of experiment in Europe, particularly by the Italian scientists Luigi Galvani and his nephew, Giovanni Aldini.

In November 1818, in the anatomy room of Glasgow University, then in the High Street, Ure carried out a series of experiments on the body of a freshly hanged murderer, Matthew Clydesdale. A sensationalised account was fabricated by Peter Mackenzie, who wrote that when the electrodes were applied to the naked body of Clydesdale, his eyes shot open, he got to his feet, pointed accusingly at Ure and began to walk. The dead man would have walked through the door of the anatomy room if the presiding Professor Jeffray had not plunged a scalpel in his throat. Meanwhile, all the spectators ran screaming from the room shouting, 'Blasphemy, blasphemy!'

It was all nonsense, of course. Ure's own account tells a very different story. To start with, he had drained the corpse of blood with the incisions needed for the insertion of the electrodes. And while the eyes and mouth did open, the face did distort, the chest did heave and then fall, the belly protruded and then collapsed and his arms and legs did thrash briefly, at no stage did Matthew Clydesdale ever get to his feet and attempt to walk out of the room. The reaction that seemed to excite the audience most was when Ure made an electrical arc between the spine and the left elbow and the fingers of the left hand began to move as if playing a ghostly tune on a violin.

Andrew Ure published his own account in the *Journal of Science and the Arts* in 1819, and in it he notes that 'several of the spectators were forced to leave the apartment from terror or sickness, and one gentleman fainted'. But most, like good medical men, stayed, fascinated by the effects of electricity on the human body and keen to ask Ure many questions about his pioneering work. In 1821 he wrote his first book, *Dictionary of Chemistry*, now considered one of the key documents from the Enlightenment in Glasgow.

The Scottish Enlightenment as a whole was the direct descendant of the Books of Discipline compiled by John Knox, Andrew Melville and the reformers of the sixteenth century. By the early decades of the eighteenth century, mass literacy and the concomitant development of education – Scotland had five universities (two in Aberdeen) compared to England's two – produced a stream of original thinkers, scientists, historians, engineers and philosophers.

Much of this creativity was concentrated in Edinburgh, and Glasgow's role in the Enlightenment is often underestimated. The historical reality is that the two men who held the chair of Moral Philosophy at Glasgow University in the mid eighteenth century exerted an enormous influence over the greatest minds in this period of remarkable intellectual flowering.

Much less well known than he deserves to be, Francis Hutcheson was an Irish minister appointed Professor of Moral Philosophy at Glasgow in 1729. The first to lecture in English rather than in Latin, he was a brilliant, passionate teacher whose influence was inspirational. Central to Hutcheson's thinking was a notion of *sensus communis*, common sense, by which he meant something that was commonly shared. He defined this as 'a determination to be pleased with the happiness of others and to be uneasy at their misery'. He also wrote of senses of beauty, the unconscious, morality (knowing the difference between right and wrong), honour and a sense of the ridiculous.

Listening to the lectures of Francis Hutcheson as an undergraduate in Glasgow was a man whose ideas had, and continue to have, an immense reach right across the world. Inspired by 'never to be forgotten Hutcheson', Adam Smith is best known for *An Inquiry into the Nature and Causes of the Wealth of Nations*. It laid the foundations of the study of economics and showed how his exposition of the interaction of mutual self-interest and competition can lead to prosperity. Politicians in particular have interpreted Smith to suit wherever they stand on the spectrum from right to left. Best to let him speak for himself. Here is his famous dictum:

> It is not from the benevolence of the butcher, the brewer, or the baker, that we expect our dinner, but from their

> regard to their own interest. We address ourselves not to their humanity but to their self-love, and never talk to them of our own necessities but of their advantages.

This extract, much quoted by those on the right wing of politics, is often interpreted as intellectual backing for their positions, a succinct statement of the operation of selfishness. But, in fact, Adam Smith would not have recognised such an interpretation. Here is the first sentence of his earlier work, *The Theory of Moral Sentiments*:

> However selfish soever man may be supposed, there are evidently some principles in his nature, which interest him in the fortunes of others, and render their happiness necessary to him, though he derive nothing from it except the pleasure of seeing it.

So while it might be assumed by some that people are innately selfish, Smith argues that experience suggests otherwise. People derive pleasure from seeing the happiness of others because human beings are social creatures: we care about others, and their condition can give us pleasure or pain. It is only through our senses, through putting ourselves in their shoes, what Smith calls empathy, that we acquire knowledge of their sentiments.

Adam Smith was appointed to succeed Francis Hutcheson as Professor of Moral Philosophy at Glasgow University in 1752, and *The Theory of Moral Sentiments* was a distillation of the lectures he gave to the students who crowded into the buildings off the High Street. Part of his appeal as a teacher was Smith's awareness of current affairs, of developments happening in Glasgow, Scotland and the wider world. As the city hummed with business and ships unloaded cargoes on the Clyde quays and merchants and manufacturers made a great deal of money, Smith was uneasy.

He loathed slavery in all its forms and was alarmed at the conditions of the working poor in early industrial capitalism, and he spent dozens of pages in *The Wealth of Nations* detailing the virtues of public education. Smith saw it as essential in countering the dehumanising effects of factory work and also in cultivating a civic consciousness amongst the working classes.

Adam Smith also worried about political apathy and encouraged people to keep an eye on unscrupulous political actors who would use government to their personal advantage. Education was a civic tool in this sense because workers and consumers needed to be citizens too. Smith devoted the longest section of *The Wealth of Nations* to ideas on public services, progressive taxation and, in particular, taxes on luxury goods. This was political thought some distance ahead of its time – and uncongenial reading for those on the right wing of modern politics who claim Smith as philosophical backing for their way of seeing the world.

Although politicians in recent times have turned to Adam Smith's *Wealth of Nations* for a philosophical justification of their beliefs and actions, there is no question that *Theory of Moral Sentiments* was in fact his defining work. As we move forward into an era when global problems such as climate change demand global solutions, it should become required reading for all of the world's politicians.

11

New Glasgow

By the early eighteenth century, Old Glasgow had nucleated around two focal points. Where the Trongate, the Saltmarket, the Gallowgate and the lower part of the High Street all met was Glasgow Cross. This area of the old town expanded as far as the Clyde, as well as to the east and west. The older, smaller town on the higher ground was built up around the cathedral, its precincts and the upper High Street.

As wealth began to flow into Glasgow from the proceeds of the Atlantic trade, the Tobacco Lords looked mainly to the west for land to build grand houses and lay out large, manicured gardens. Some were palatial. In 1711 work began on Shawfield House for the MP, banker and slave owner, Daniel Campbell, and it stood at the foot of what is now Glassford Street. In 1725 it was attacked and badly damaged by rioters protesting about an increase in the tax on malted barley, the main ingredient of beer. Long demolished, all that remembers the house now is a plaque on the wall of a branch of Café Nero that reminds passers-by that Prince Charles lodged at Shawfield House in 1745. It may be where he met his much-loved bidie-in, Clementina Walkinshaw.

In 1751 the old West Port was dismantled and that opened the way to development to the west of the old town. The renowned Edinburgh architects Robert and James Adam designed the new Trades Hall in Glassford Street, a new infirmary near the cathedral, the Corn Exchange in Hope Street and the Assembly Rooms in Ingram Street. The first of these is magnificent, and in addition to being the headquarters of the Trades House of Glasgow (what was the craft guild of the city as opposed to the merchants' association), it has become an upmarket wedding venue. The Corn Exchange was used by hundreds of grain merchants, flour millers and importers. After being converted into a bank, it was demolished after the Second World War. The Assembly Rooms in Ingram Street did not last as long, less than a century, before it was pulled down. As ever, Glasgow did not hesitate to change, sweeping away grand buildings in pursuit of a better or at least a different future. The relentless process of renewal was unceasing.

Development also began to creep over the farmland to the south of the Clyde. The Trades Hall owned land there, along with Hutcheson's Hospital (originally built to house old and infirm Glasgow merchants and a free school for poor boys) and the old barony of the Gorbals. From the second half of the eighteenth century all three began to feu land to builders. There were conditions attached. The street plan had to be a grid and the housing would not be grand, but consist of four-storey tenements. The exception to this was Carlton Place, a riverside terrace on the south bank that faced the old town. It was designed in 1802 by Peter Nicolson, and it was 200 years ahead of its time. Carlton Terrace was the showpiece for what the developer, John Laurie, hoped would grow into a high-class residential suburb, which he modestly dubbed Laurieston. The heavy industry that clustered on the banks of the Clyde, with all its racket and pollution, persuaded affluent Glaswegians to look for houses in the West End. Unlike Paris or London, central Glasgow's riverbank was heavily industrialised until trade was diverted and the shipyards began to close. The developments of the late twentieth and early twenty-first centuries have changed its character radically. While Laurieston House is being restored, the rest of Carlton Terrace is still a mess.

Developers also turned their attentions to the old town. Two key figures were the architect David Hamilton and his partner, James Cleland. They refurbished the Tolbooth, and it was used as a warehouse after the burgh council had moved to a splendid neoclassical building in the Saltmarket, what is now the Justiciary Buildings, a complex of courtrooms and offices. The main block of the Tolbooth was demolished in 1921, leaving the monumental old steeple freestanding, dominating Glasgow Cross.

David Hamilton was centrally involved in the layout and building of the new town to the west of the old. The rectilinear grid was relieved by well-designed squares: St Andrew's, George, St Enoch's and Exchange Square. Their harmonious, uniform appearance reflected an intense period of building work over three to four decades. By the 1980s this first area of expansion had become known as the Merchant City.

Glasgow's drumlins were no discouragement to architects and developers. From the fairly flat site immediately to the west of the old town, the ground rises gently to Blythswood Hill and Garnethill. Sauchiehall Street was first to be opened up for housing; Bath Street followed in 1802. St Vincent Street leads up to Blythswood Square on the long summit of a drumlin. To the north, Garnethill got its name as a tribute to Professor Thomas Garnett, an English doctor and philosopher who set up an observatory on the hill. It is believed that the original grid plan was designed by James Craig, the winner of a competition to create a layout for Edinburgh's New Town in 1767. Glasgow's collective sense of itself only allows this as a possibility and not an absolute fact. What is certain is the influence of the concept of the grid plan in the USA, where expanding cities like New York and Boston adopted it.

Perhaps the Park district, set on Woodlands Hill, another drumlin, is one of the most pleasing developments in what became known as the West End. Beside Kelvingrove Park, several terraces cluster around Park Circus, an oval rather than a circle with a beautiful garden in the centre. The surrounding streets are wide and the aspect in all directions is open. Because of the drumlins, Glasgow is a city where the hills and the countryside around it are often in view, and the sense of enclosure of cities like London and Paris, the centres of both built on flat sites, is absent. Although the townhouses and terraced flats in the Park district are mostly four or five storeys, there is no sense of them being overpowering. When the building work was completed in 1863, there was great demand. During the later twentieth century, many of the larger townhouses were converted for office use, but more recently companies have begun to move out and the residents return. This is a discernible pattern of change across the centre of Glasgow, and especially in the West End. The habit of remote working, dispensing with the need for large offices, forced by the COVID-19 pandemic, can only accelerate this process.

12

Clyde Goes Forth

Industry and commerce require movement in two directions: in and out. As Glasgow's economy began to expand, the mills, factories and forges needed coal – and lots of it. Horses could only pull so much, and carts could never be big enough to transport the huge quantities of fuel required as business boomed. Other materials such as iron ore and timber were also needed in bulk. And once factories, mills and forges had burned all that coal and manufactured whatever they sold, these products needed to go out, to get to market or to customers. And all of this needed to be done as quickly and as cheaply as possible, and in bulk.

In an age before railways and long before roads ceased to be muddy, potholed tracks (until quite recently), canals and barges were the answer. In the Midlands of England, the cradle of the Industrial Revolution, canals were quickly dug and immediately heavily used. In Glasgow, the Tobacco Lords were very enthusiastic about a proposal to dig a canal that would link the Clyde with the Forth. This would save time, money, ships and lives. The problem was that the sole means of getting bulk goods from Glasgow to the Firth of Forth, the eastern coasts of Britain, the North Sea and the European ports beyond was a long and hazardous voyage around the top of Scotland. Once around Cape Wrath, merchant ships would have to navigate the treacherous, fast-moving riptides of the Pentland Firth, waters that were especially dangerous.

In 1768 the Westminster parliament passed an act enabling the construction of the Forth and Clyde Canal, and the search for backers began. Costs were estimated at £150,000 and work was soon underway. But the project immediately ran into difficulties. The canal would have to be cut through no fewer than twenty different sorts of rock formations and thirty-nine locks would be needed along its thirty-five-mile length to cope with variable ground levels. Costs spiralled. Workers were difficult to recruit and unreliable. When the squads of navvies (canals were sometimes called 'navigations' and those who dug them were known as 'navigators') began to work at Dullatur Bog, near Kilsyth, they found that the ground was highly unstable and very difficult to excavate. And there was the added problem of history. The navvies kept uncovering the bodies of Covenanters killed at the Battle of Kilsyth in 1645. There had been great slaughter as the Marquis of Montrose's Highlanders had cut down hundreds of fleeing men as they floundered in the marshes. And the navvies did not only find skeletons. Many of the bodies had been partly preserved in the anaerobic conditions. Apparently one cavalry trooper was uncovered still astride his horse. And this was pick, shovel and barrow work, where such macabre discoveries would have been up close and personal.

Of course, the initial estimate was far below what the new canal would actually cost. The cash ran out in 1775 and work was halted. But history came full circle from the royalist victory at Kilsyth in 1645. More money was raised 'arising from the forfeited estates' of the Jacobite landowners who had found themselves on the losing side after 1746.

By 28 July 1790 investors and industrialists were celebrating. Despite all the difficulties, the Forth and Clyde Canal had been completed. Running from near Grangemouth in the east to Bowling on the north bank of the Clyde, its route happened to follow the line of the Antonine Wall, and at Kirkintilloch the canal was very close to the Roman remains. It had taken twenty-two years of back-breaking work and great financial risk (which never paid off since the shareholders made no money), but the canal did greatly facilitate the movement of goods and raw materials, and was, incidentally, well used by fishing boats moving from the North Sea to the Atlantic as they followed the herring shoals.

Almost as important to Glasgow was the Monkland Canal. It was routed from the Lanarkshire coalfields into the heart of the city to keep it reliably supplied with fuel, and in bulk so that it could be stockpiled in summer for domestic consumption. It was to run from the pits around Calderbank and into the centre from the southeast. Work began in 1771 and quickly ran into problems. One of the most extreme concerned the source of water. It was supposed to come from Hogganfield Loch and any streams that were not already draining into the Forth and Clyde Canal, but there was not enough and levels could drop sharply. And, as usual, costs increased and the money ran out. The shortfall (and the water problem) was solved by a plan to link the Monkland Canal to the Forth and Clyde. This was thought to be potentially very lucrative, investors were attracted, and by 1791 the junction was opened at Maryhill. And business did indeed boom. As more coal was extracted from the North Lanarkshire pits, it became cheaper, and more steam-powered mills and factories could make a profit as a virtuous circle began to turn. In 1793 the Monkland Canal shipped 50,000 tonnes of coal, but by 1850 that figure had soared to a million. When iron ore was found in quantity near Glasgow, short branches of the canal were dug to Calder Iron Works,

Gartsherrie Iron Works, Langloan Iron Works and Dundyvan Iron Works.

But it was a relatively brief heyday. By the 1860s the railway network had extended its tentacles, and suppliers to industry were shifting to the faster and cheaper transport that trains offered. Barge traffic declined drastically as roads also began to improve, and by the early twentieth century, few boats rippled the dark surfaces of the canals that had once fed Glasgow's industry. Much of the Monkland Canal has disappeared, some of it buried under the line of the M8 motorway, and only a short section now runs through the Summerlee Country Park in North Lanarkshire.

Nowadays the Forth and Clyde Canal is used for recreation, a place where people like to cruise for short distances through the Central Belt in slow boats, or paddle kayaks for a few miles. Walkers use the towpaths and try to dodge the cyclists who have every possible gadget on their expensive bikes except a bell. They can marvel at sculptor Andy Scott's hundred-feet-high horse-head sculptures, the Kelpies, and have a go on the world's only rotating boat lift, the Falkirk Wheel, that connects the Forth and Clyde Canal to the Union Canal. The Claypits nature reserve is full of wild birds, roe deer and dragonflies.

Port Dundas was a terminus of the Forth and Clyde Canal, and Speirs Wharf housed the offices, grain stores and warehouses of the Forth and Clyde Navigation Company. In 1989 these imposing blond sandstone buildings, with views over the city centre, were converted into loft-style flats and a private leisure centre. A preserved section of the canal sits in front of them. As ever, Glasgow moved on.

13

Drouthy City

As the eighteenth century turned to the nineteenth, Glasgow expanded, its industry thrummed, new streets were laid out, housing built and whatever seemed to lie in the path of progress was summarily, unhesitatingly swept aside. The city's face seemed to be set resolutely to the future. Except for one absolute essential. The city had no reliable supply of clean water, something that seems remarkable in retrospect. Well into the 1840s, Glasgow continued to depend on medieval sources of water. A series of springs, most of them in the old town, supplied the only access to clean water for the mushrooming population. The West Port Well, Bell's Wynd Well, the Spout Mouth and the Lady Well were all used on a daily basis. One enterprising individual, William Harley, owned a small estate around what is now Charing Cross and on his property were several springs. Most days he trundled barrels of his water into the city and sold it for a 'halfpenny a stoup' or a flagon. It was said that Haley made around £4,000 a year, a substantial sum.

In 1806 James Watt and Thomas Telford proposed a radical solution to what was becoming an acute problem. Water would be pumped from the Clyde up to a large reservoir at Dalmarnock. From there it would be filtered and piped back down into Glasgow for public consumption. But the scheme was abandoned when it became clear that the river was too heavily polluted, mostly with the city's own sewage. In 1846 the Gorbals Gravitation Water Company began to supply water, but only to the south side of the Clyde. The primitive water supply from the wells in the old town and elsewhere in the city was not only inadequate, it could also be dangerous. Cholera epidemics in 1832 and 1848 claimed the lives of over 7,000 people.

Eventually, a man with much-needed vision and determination emerged. At the age of only forty-one, Robert Stewart became lord provost and immediately engaged the services of the highly respected English engineer John Bateman to come up with a proposal. After some months of research, travel and consultation, he came to the conclusion that a famous Highland loch would be able to supply Glasgow with enough clean water. With the publication of *The Lady of the Lake* in 1810, Walter Scott had made the name of Loch Katrine well known across the western world and sparked the beginning of tourism as visitors came north to see for themselves where the poem's heroines and heroes had met. The loch lies twenty-six miles to the north of Glasgow, and the process of bringing its water to the city would be very difficult and costly, but Bateman was adamant: 'Loch Katrine seems to stand alone in the field. No other will meet the requirements of the case.'

Despite the objections of the water-peddlers, the tight-fisted burghers and landowners around the loch, Lord Provost Stewart was resolute. The sole sensible objection came from chemist Dr Frederick Penny of the Andersonian Institute, the forerunner of Strathclyde University, when he pointed out that the soft water of Loch Katrine running through long runs of lead pipes could become toxic. Therefore Bateman made sure that lead was avoided where possible. The dissenters were finally silenced when the lord provost wheeled out the great engineer Isambard Kingdom Brunel, who pronounced that 'the Loch Katrine project is decidedly to be preferred'.

The twenty-six-mile-long pipeline from the loch that led to a huge reservoir at Mugdock, north of Milngavie, was a spectacular feat of Victorian engineering. The water was carried across twenty-two aqueducts and through two stone-clad tunnels, each one a mile and a half long. Gravity was of course the governing force. Loch Katrine lay at a much higher altitude than the reservoir at Mugdock, but the terrain between rose and fell, sometimes dramatically. 'Drop' is what plumbers look for when supplying water to and from a tank, or whatever source they are using, and pressure is also vitally important. An enormous volume of water lay behind the pipeline and its pressure had to be controlled with a very gradual drop of only ten inches per mile.

When Queen Victoria opened the Loch Katrine supply in October 1859, there was a whiff of sniffiness in the air as she noted Glasgow's 'vast population which is rapidly increasing'. The *London Illustrated News* appeared neither to know nor care that Glaswegians would no longer live in the shadow of cholera, choosing instead to mourn the exploitation of the lake of *The Lady of the Lake*. It griped that 'a provincial city four hundred miles off, wholly occupied with manufacturers, merchants and shipbuilders with hardly the pretence of a West End, or an aristocracy . . . had received the waters of several noble lakes for the supply of its inhabitants'. Oh, dear.

Despite the cost, ingenuity and immense labour, Loch Katrine could not supply enough fresh water. The city needed a staggering 50 million gallons a day (which begs the question: how did it manage before the scheme opened?) and John Bateman's pipeline brought only 40 million. In 1885 nearby Loch Arklet, which lay between Loch Katrine and Loch Lomond, was tapped. Its supply made up the shortfall, and to cope with the added volume, a second reservoir was built at Craigmaddie, near Mugdock.

Sadly, the man who made it all happen, Lord Provost Stewart, was felled by a heart attack at the young age of fifty-six. In 1872 the Water Commissioners of Glasgow dedicated an elaborate fountain in Kelvingrove Park to Stewart and his achievement. The statue on top is not him but, strangely and inappropriately, Ellen Douglas, the imaginary Lady of the Lake in Walter Scott's poem, and the stonework is decorated with scenes from the Trossachs. After years of being vandalised, it was restored in 2009, on the 150th anniversary of the opening of the pipeline from the loch. Rather than commemorating someone who never existed, Glasgow Council should have taken the opportunity to replace her with one of its greatest lord provosts.

14

The Polis

In 2021 the Advertising Standards Authority warned the Metropolitan Police to cease and desist. A knowledgeable, loyal and long-serving police officer from Glasgow had pointed out that the Met had repeatedly claimed to be the first modern, municipal police force in Britain. This was not true. The City of Glasgow Police had been formed in 1779 (fifty years before Sir Robert Peel's Metropolitan Police Force was founded and based in Scotland Yard), and after years of lobbying, parliament had been persuaded to pass the Glasgow Police Act of 1800. The ASA insisted on a written undertaking from the Metropolitan Police never to repeat this false claim.

The derivation of the term 'police' is from the Greek word *polis*, pronounced much in the same way that 'police' is pronounced in Glasgow. And it was that derivation on the minds of those who set up the first municipal police force. Polis means city, and it implied a role for the polis in maintaining public order in the polis. In fact, the Glasgow polis pioneered what was known as preventive policing. In 1788 the bailies (or the magistrates of the town council, later Glasgow Corporation) decreed that the polis would be overseen by a Watch Committee also known as Commissioners. The constables would wear black uniforms and badges inscribed with 'Police', and they would also put up a bond of

£50 as a guarantee of proper conduct. Only eight of them at first, the polis maintained twenty-four-hour patrols of the city's streets to prevent crime and detect any who might have committed a crime.

By 1800 three sergeants and six constables had set up their headquarters, the first police station, in the Session House of the Laigh Kirk in the Trongate. Their daily patrols, organised in shifts, were supplemented by watchmen in brown coats and with numbers on their backs. These men stood at fixed points, mostly street corners, each with a lantern on a long stave, as the constables patrolled the streets. By 1846 the city police had merged with the Gorbals, Calton and Anderston burgh police to create a force of 360 men. By that time, a long tradition of Highlanders as Glasgow policemen had begun. They were known as the Teuchter polis. Well fed 'meal mountains', they were also called, and much valued as 'big, steady lads' who could keep order without fuss or fluster. Dr John Aitken, a police commissioner, was very proud of a 'force so large and overwhelming that it would drive iniquity out of the city as though by a hurricane'.

And by the 1920s there was a great deal of iniquity on Glasgow's streets, and a different, unwelcome sort of hurricane was blowing through them. In the East End and the Southside of the city, razor gangs became active, so called because of their weapon of choice, a pen-knife style cutthroat razor that could be easily concealed in an inside pocket. At least two factors seemed to be at work. Since the tragic devastation of the Irish Famine in the 1840s, immigration had created tensions in what had been an overwhelmingly Protestant city. The Billy Boys were based in Bridgeton and led by Billy Fullerton, a member of the British Union of Fascists with close links to Oswald Mosley. The gang actually took their name from King William of Orange, King Billy, and a loyalist marching song, 'The Billy Boys'. They had a paramilitary aspect, dressing in similar clothes, usually dark suits, and took to marching through Catholic areas on saints' days and other festivals. The Billy Boys also began attending Glasgow Rangers matches and their song became part of the crowd's repertoire.

Deliberately provocative, the marches produced a Catholic reaction. The oddly named Norman Conks (it came from the Norman Conquerors, which in turn derived from their base in Norman Street, also in Bridgeton) supplied the main opposition, often reinforced by their allies, the Calton Tongs. Unusually, the Norman Conks had women in their ranks. Unlike the Billy Boys, the Catholic gang had been active since the 1880s and were known as a penny mob. This label was coined by the Glasgow newspapers after the police courts took to fining arrested gang members a penny a head instead of imprisoning them. Another, much more gory coining at that time came from the St Mungie's Warriors. In street fights, and when they had captured an opposing gang member, they used their razors to slash their mouths from corner to ear, creating the Glasgow Smile.

Economics also played a determinant part in the rise of the razor gangs. Between 1930 and 1935, in the wake of the Wall Street Crash, the Depression had seen unemployment in Glasgow rise to between 25 per cent and 33 per cent. And there was acute overcrowding in the tenements of the city centre. The housing stock was poor, badly maintained, with outside or communal toilets, often no running water and widespread rat infestation.

The polis confronted the gangs in the streets, but they were often outnumbered. They employed a series of informers, usually barmen in the city's pubs, who could supply warnings of activity, but it was not until Sir Percy Sillitoe became chief constable in 1931 that the problem of street violence abated. In Sheffield, he had encouraged and authorised the use of 'reasonable force' by his officers, and in Glasgow he actively recruited Highlanders, those 'big, steady lads' mentioned earlier, who often towered over gang members. Sillitoe also introduced the band of black-and-white dicing for police hats, having borrowed the design from the Glengarries of the Scottish regiments. It became known as 'the Sillitoe tartan'. Short-wave wireless radios were issued to officers on the beat who had previously relied on police boxes to contact their stations and each other, and more vehicles were brought into use to speed up response times. By the mid 1930s, the polis had regained control of the streets, and Sillitoe eventually moved on to become head of MI5 during the Second World War.

The outbreak of war saw a reduction in gang warfare for a spell, but trouble broke out again in the late 1960s. The inner city slums had largely disappeared, but groups of young men began to seek the adrenaline rush of violence in the peripheral housing estates. In 1968 the singer Frankie Vaughan, who had experienced gang culture in Liverpool as a poor young Jewish boy, came to Glasgow to talk to the young people involved. He played a concert and asked rival gang leaders to shake hands and give up their weapons. Three binfuls of knives were handed in, and Vaughan kept returning to the city to reinforce his efforts.

In the decades that followed, the situation worsened. There were at least 170 gangs in the city, and instead of cutthroat razors, large knives and even machetes were the weapons of choice. Glasgow became known as 'the murder capital of Europe'. In 2005, after Scotland had been named the most violent country in the developed world (there had been 137 homicides in one year, with forty-one in Glasgow alone)

Police Scotland, the successor to the Glasgow police force, set up the Violence Reduction Unit. In addition to law enforcement, the police began to link with social services and the education authorities to deal with the root causes of violent crime. This public health approach, underpinned by the belief that all forms of violence are preventable, has been highly effective, with a 35 per cent reduction in homicide figures, and the numbers of young people roaming the streets seeking the companionship of gangs and the thrill of confrontation has decreased substantially.

15

Seawards the Great Ships

On 9 April 1962, in the Santa Monica Civic Auditorium, the actors George Hamilton and Glynis Johns, with some awkwardness and hesitation, opened an envelope and read out the name of the winner of the Oscar for the best short live action film of the year. It was *Seawards the Great Ships*. Directed by Hilary Harris and written by Cliff Hanley and John Grierson, the pioneering Scottish documentary maker, its story of post-war shipbuilding on the banks of the Clyde was unintentionally valedictory. Interviews with shipyard workers apparently had to be scripted because the men used too many swear words. The film opens with a stunning sequence of close-ups of the launch of several of the Great Ships, the accompanying soundtrack a series of clips of cut-glass female voices: 'I name this ship . . .' The beautifully shot footage captures something both elemental and elegiac. After the months of clattering, hammering, the riveting of steel plates, the lightning sparks of the welders and the supporting scaffolding finally peeling away, the huge hulls glide into the water with heart-stopping elegance, released from the racket of the shipyard into their element. The ships are stately and silent in the river until the massive chains dragging behind bring them slowly to a halt.

It has all gone now. No longer do ranks of tall cranes and busy shipyards line the riverbank. No longer are hundreds of ships launched each year, and no longer do the thousands of men who built them rush out of the yard gates when the hooter sounds. The term 'Clydebuilt' is no longer anything more than a historical label. And yet the glory days of shipbuilding, that lasted for more than a century, might never have come about if Lord North had been a better prime minister and George III a more inclusive monarch. If the American War of Independence had not ended with the loss of the thirteen colonies, the parish minister of Greenock might not have written in 1793 that:

> with respect to shipbuilding, it may not be improper to mention that formerly all the large vessels belonging to Clyde were built in America: but since the Americans established their independence, shipbuilding has gone on briskly in the ports of Clyde.

Until the later nineteenth century, mainly sailing ships were built on the river, the most famous and fastest being the *Cutty Sark*, named after a character in Robert Burns' *Tam o' Shanter* and now permanently berthed at Greenwich in London. But the industry did not really begin to expand significantly until Robert Napier started to build not ships but engines. Steam engines were the future, and in 1838 Napier was commissioned to build warships for the Royal Navy. Two years later Samuel Cunard ordered four transatlantic paddle steamers and Napier subcontracted the making of the hulls to other yards on the river. A new and much more efficient cylindrical boiler that needed less coal and made room for more cargo was invented, probably by the Glasgow engineer James Howden, sometime around 1860. From that moment shipbuilding on the Clyde became big business.

In the second half of the nineteenth century famous firms were founded, among them John Brown & Company, Fairfield Shipbuilding and Engineering, Yarrow Shipbuilders, Barclay Curle, Lithgows, A. & J. Inglis and Harland & Wolff and many others. And this gathering boom in production had an electric effect on Glasgow's manufacturing industry. Here is Charles Oakley from the Board of Trade, writing in 1937:

> There are many great firms in the district that specialize in making such major auxiliaries as engines, oilers, pumps, valves, fans, ventilating plant, davits, refrigerating plant and lifeboats . . . Accordingly many firms have established factories to supply the ships with the particular article in which they specialize . . . It has been estimated that for every worker employed in a shipyard, two others are employed in industries supplying the materials for ship construction.

Business boomed to levels that now seem unimaginable. In the decade before the outbreak of the First World War, Glasgow saw an unprecedented number of launches. In 1913 alone the Clyde yards built almost 400 ships, some of them very large, very expensive and very prestigious. For the Cunard Line, John Brown & Company constructed the *Lusitania*, the world's largest passenger ship; her fastest crossing of the Atlantic was in 1909 (taking four days, sixteen hours and forty minutes). In 1915 the great ship was sunk off the Irish coast by a German submarine with the loss of 1,197 passengers and crew. The Clyde was so busy that workers flocked to the yards and the factories around them from all over Britain, and much to Birmingham's annoyance, Glasgow took to calling itself the Second City of the Empire.

Oil was ultimately the Clyde's undoing. After the First World War, it began to replace coal as fuel, and the yards had to scramble to keep up with rivals in the USA and Europe. When the Great Depression hit the world economy after 1929, Charles Oakley observed that in the 1930s the Clyde's shipyards made a faster recovery because owners had the resources to invest in new methods during the periods of enforced downtime. He pointed out that in 1936 the yards had launched ninety-one ships of all kinds, from Admiralty cruisers to dredgers and coastal motorboats. And from John Brown's slipway the *Queen Mary* and the *Queen Elizabeth* both glided down into the river.

After the Second World War, the badly mauled German and Japanese yards benefited, like much of their battered industry, from being completely rebuilt and fitted out with the latest technology. The Clyde fought back: in 1953 there were nineteen yards still working, eight on the north bank, eleven on the south, with Harland & Wolff in Govan at one end and Scott's Shipbuilding & Engineering in Scotstoun at the other. But it proved to be a post-war high point, and business slowly declined. The last hurrah, the last champagne bottle cracked on a big, prestigious ship, was smashed into the hull of the *Queen Elizabeth 2* (*QE2*), in 1967.

The yards were failing fast, and mergers and nationalisation failed to save them. Perhaps the last act of defiance took place in 1971. Five yards, including John Brown & Company and Yarrow's, were folded into the Upper Clyde Shipyards (UCS). But that too failed, threatening 8,500 jobs. However, rather than meekly accepting redundancy, Jimmy Reid and Jimmy Airlie famously led a 'work-in'. Both men were members of the Communist Party and determined to assert workers' rights rather than accept the decisions of their bosses. In a speech made to a crowd of 30,000 on Glasgow Green,

Reid reminded them and the UCS workers that the world was watching.

> There will be no hooliganism, there will be no vandalism, there will be no bevvying [drinking] and [Edward] Heath, [Prime Minister] should take note that unless he and his colleagues are prepared to meet the urgent social needs of the people then this eruption will engulf both him and his government.

A few months later, the work-in collapsed – but the Heath government did not survive a confrontation with another group of trade unions, the miners, and lost office in 1974.

A pale ghost of what it once was, Clyde shipbuilding has all but disappeared. The mighty industry that employed many tens of thousands, that made the sleek windjammer, the *Cutty Sark*, the luxurious *Lusitania*, great battleships like HMS *Hood* and HMS *Repulse* and the three queens, *Mary*, *Elizabeth* and *Elizabeth 2*, is now much reduced. There are two BAE systems yards at Govan and Scotstoun turning out vessels for the Royal Navy and one other small yard. The latter finds it too difficult to build an inter-island ferry. A sad end to an old song of the Clyde.

16

They Belong to Glasgow

The glass-walled bridge across Argyle Street that carries the platforms of Central Station remembers a long wave of immigrants who fetched up in Glasgow. It is known as the Hielanman's Umbrella because it was used as a rendezvous by emigrants from the Highlands and Islands, a dry place to meet in the city centre, usually at the weekends, before going to the pub, the dance hall or both. It was also a place where a cigarette could be lit, Gaelic was spoken, and echoes of a very different life could be heard.

Emigration from the Highlands began in earnest after the government-sponsored genocide that followed the defeat of Prince Charles and his Jacobite army at Culloden in 1746. In what Gaels called *Am Bliadhna nan Creach*, the Year of Pillaging, when herds of cattle were stolen, farmhouses burned, men summarily executed and women raped, many Highlanders fled south to find work or passage to North America, or even further afield. When landlords initiated the Highland Clearances in the nineteenth century, more came south and found work not only in the police force but in domestic service, and men with seagoing skills were employed by the Clyde Trust. It managed the river, making sure the shipping channel was properly dredged, and also administered the quays, docks and other maritime facilities. Highlanders also found employment in the ferry services around the Clyde, and the boats became known as the Skye Navy. As with most groups of immigrants, especially those who did not have much English, only Gaelic, they clustered in communities. Partick, or *Partaig*, was home to many Gaels.

At the same time as the Irish people suffered appallingly from the Famine, a similar blight affected the Highlands, and in 1846 and 1847, there was a surge in emigration, many coming to Glasgow. The 1881 Census counted 11,000 Gaelic speakers in the city; by 1901 there were 18,500. Despite a good deal of prejudice, some of which has not entirely abated, Highlanders did integrate in Glasgow, and were largely welcomed. The same could not be said for the second substantial group who arrived in the city in the middle of the nineteenth century.

Between 1845 and 1852 Ireland was in the grip of *an Gorta Mór*, the Great Hunger, a catastrophe without parallel in Europe. The potato crop on which ordinary people depended was devastated by blight, and more than a million died of starvation. Two million more emigrated, many of them making the short passage across the North Channel to the Firth of Clyde and on to Glasgow. At its peak in 1848, emigration became a flood as a thousand Irish refugees disembarked each week on the Clyde quays, and between January and April that year a staggering 48,860 came. It was the largest and most rapid influx of new people in Scotland's history, and in the Census of 1851, the enumerators counted more than 200,000 who had been born in Ireland. They were desperate, fleeing from the famine in droves, and the new immigrants, willing to accept lower wages to put food on the table for their hungry families, often priced native Scots out of low-skilled manual work. It was a demographic shock that drew uncharitable, un-Christian reactions. Here is a report from the 1871 Census:

> The immigration of such a number of people from the lowest class and with no education will have a bad effect on the population. So far, living amongst the Scots does not seem to have improved the Irish, but the native Scots who live among the Irish have got worse. It is difficult to imagine the effect the Irish immigrants will have upon the morals and habits of the Scottish people.

These seeds of prejudice soon flourished and led to conflict and division, and these became, and continued to be, most visible on winter Saturday afternoons as sectarianism ribboned through the history of Scotland's two greatest football clubs. Celtic FC was founded in November 1887 to help alleviate poverty in Glasgow's East End parishes. It was the initiative of Brother Walfrid, an Irish priest who had been encouraged by the example of Hibernian FC: 'A football club will be formed for the maintenance of dinner clubs for the children and the unemployed.' The club recruited players from the Irish immigrant community in Edinburgh and the east of Scotland. Celtic played their first fixture against Rangers in 1888, and won 5–2. Support for each club began to polarise around the immigrant Irish Catholic community and the native Scottish Protestants. In the middle of the seventeenth century blue had become the colour of militant Protestantism when officers in the Covenanter armies began to wear blue sashes to distinguish themselves, and green was forever associated with Ireland, the Emerald Isle.

Sir John Primrose was a wealthy Glasgow merchant who became lord provost in 1902 and chairman of Rangers Football Club between 1912 and 1923. The same year Primrose took over, the Belfast shipyard Harland & Wolff bought three yards on the Clyde at Govan and brought over many skilled workers with them from Ulster. These men were almost all Protestants and Unionists, and they began to support their local club, Glasgow Rangers. The arrival of these immigrants also saw support of a different sort increase. Many joined the Orange Lodges. These affiliations were made more pointed because of the introduction of a Home Rule Bill for Ireland in 1912, which the Ulster Protestants vigorously opposed, and some lodges in the north began to arm themselves. Although the outbreak of the First World War stalled this proposed legislation and diverted all sorts of energies and enmities elsewhere, it had the effect of making the division between Catholics and Protestants in Scotland sharper. At Rangers football club, Sir John Primrose supported the policy of not signing Catholic players.

The equivalent was not adopted by Celtic FC, and throughout the later twentieth century Protestants were amongst their most distinguished players, the likes of Kenny Dalglish and Danny McGrain. And the club's most successful manager, Jock Stein, was also a Protestant.

Since the end of the Second World War, and particularly after the signing of the Good Friday Agreement in 1998 that brought an end to the violence in Northern Ireland, both clubs have come together to stamp out sectarianism, banning inflammatory songs such as 'The Billy Boys' and inappropriate salutes and chants, and discouraging the waving of the Irish tricolour and the Union Jack. And on the signing of the Catholic player Mo Johnston by Rangers in 1989, the policy introduced during the chairmanship of Sir John Primrose effectively came to an end.

17

Rail, Steam and Speed

On 4 May 1987 a strange funeral cortege passed through the centre of Glasgow. It began at a disused works in Springburn where sculptor George Wyllie had built a steam locomotive out of straw. As big as a real one, it was lifted onto a low loader and followed by two open-topped buses filled with mourners. With Wyllie in a yellow overall waving out of the engine driver's cab, the cortege made a circuit of George Square, passing in front of the City Chambers before climbing the hill up St Vincent Street to Blythswood Square. After it had crossed the bridge over the M8, the low loader, its straw locomotive and the two buses arrived at Finnieston Quay and the gigantic, cantilevered crane on the riverbank. After steel hawsers were attached to each corner, the loco was lifted high into the air by the long arm and swung around. For forty-eight days it was suspended over the empty Clyde, waiting for a ship that never came. The straw steam engine was only lowered when birds started nesting in it. On 22 June, it returned to Springburn where George Wyllie set his creation alight in what he described as 'a Viking funeral'. Some of the old men watching were in tears.

Glasgow had once been a world-leading builder of steam locomotives. Its story began in 1856 when the St Rollox Works opened in Springburn, and it was soon followed by several other companies: the Queen's Park Works, the Hyde

Park Works and the Atlas Works. The supply network for these large factories rippled outwards, much as it did for the shipbuilding industry, to satellite companies in Kilmarnock, Wishaw and Motherwell where wagons, carriages and wheels were made. In 1903 three of the larger companies merged to become the North British Locomotive Company, the largest manufacturer in Europe. The NBL built engines for railway companies as far afield as the Philippines, India and China. When the First World War erupted in 1914, the Springburn works quickly switched to the production of armaments, including parts for tanks, bombs, artillery shells and mines. More than 8,000 people were employed, and so many volunteered for the armed forces that the numbers had to be restricted. One NBL man won the Victoria Cross.

In 1932 the huge Titan crane was erected on Finnieston Quay. It is 175 feet high and the lifting arm is 152 feet long. It was necessary to cantilever it with a great counterweight on the shorter end of the arm so that it could hoist locomotives weighing up to 175 tons. Like George Wyllie's straw version, these were pulled through the streets of the city centre, often by teams of Clydesdale horses, although they will have avoided going up St Vincent Street. Once in position under the crane, the locomotives had hawsers attached and were lifted up, swung around and loaded into the holds of cargo ships. It is estimated that more than 18,000 were exported from Glasgow in this way from the Finnieston Crane and six others on the Clyde. Ironically, the surviving crane that now dominates the riverside was not built in Glasgow. The tower was assembled by Cowans, Sheldon & Co. of Carlisle and the great cantilever was put together by Cleveland Bridge & Engineering of Darlington.

When the Labour Party won the general election of 1945 in a landslide, one of the first companies to be nationalised was NBL. It became part of British Rail Engineering. By the 1950s the age of steam was giving way to electric locomotives and diesel-powered trains. But, increasingly, Springburn was left behind as locos were built elsewhere. When he set alight to the straw engine in June 1987, George Wyllie spoke to an elderly woman who had been a tracer at NBL. 'We just didn't see the changes coming,' she said. 'Didn't keep up.' Many others watching the blaze were regretful, having also worked in production. In the 1930s, as a young man, Wyllie himself had worked in the busy docks around the Finnieston Crane.

In May 2018 at the Riverside Museum, an exhibition celebrating Glasgow's industrial heritage was held. The largest object on show was South Africa loco 3007. Built in 1945 in Springburn, it was still hauling wagons and carriages in South Africa until 1987. One visitor who had a particular reason for visiting left a comment: 'To see steam locos I worked on made me feel like a museum piece.' In 1961 NBL stopped all production; a year later they went into liquidation. Its powerful, elegant, impressive locomotives are preserved in museums all over the world; in Australia, New Zealand, Malaysia, France, Norway, South Africa and Japan. And instead of making and exporting objects, Glasgow now shows them off as visitor attractions replace manufacture. These places provide some jobs and stimulate economic activity, but passive has replaced active on the Glasgow quays.

Ingenuity, vision and daring entrepreneurialism were all central to Glasgow's success in making things of all kinds. One of the last and most spectacular of this collection of undoubted virtues was captured in a futuristic poster published in 1929. Against a background of what might be mountains, a loch and a river, a conventional steam train runs on conventional tracks. But above it is the future. Suspended from an overhead monorail supported by tall gantries is a sleek, aerodynamic train, not with a funnel but a propeller attached to the rounded nose. On the side of this remarkable conveyance are the letters 'GBR'. They stand for the George Bennie Railplane, and beside the speeding train that is clearly outpacing the steam loco are the words: SWIFT, SAFE, SURE.

This bullet-like train was Bennie's brainchild, even his obsession. He was a Glasgow engineer with a dream, one that was way ahead of its time. Bennie designed an engine that, he claimed, could travel at 120mph, and he wanted to build an overhead rail above the line from Glasgow to Edinburgh. The journey would take less than half an hour. In a field near Milngavie, an experimental track, 130 yards long, was constructed and a 48-seat carriage, with propellers at each end, was built. And, to some extent, it worked. The carriage seemed stable as it ran along the overhead rail, moving slowly but smoothly over the short distance. Several short and silent films were made by British Pathé News, and they showed bowler-hatted gentlemen boarding the train for a trial run. One of them, wagging his finger and explaining what was what, was clearly Bennie himself. The Railplane ran overhead the conventional LNER line, but because it travelled only 100 yards, its comparative speed could not be assessed. Those who had a brief journey in the prototype pronounced it 'somewhat noisy'. In fact, the racket of the engine and the propellers was ear-shattering. It was just as well that the Pathé films were silent.

George Bennie went bankrupt in 1935, and his great and noble venture lay rusting in the field at Milngavie until it was dismantled and sold for scrap in 1956. Bennie was one of Glasgow's most visionary engineers: monorail systems like his, although differently powered and quieter, are now in use across the world, many of them in airports. GBR was a failure, but a heroic failure.

18

Thomson and Toshie

In 1966 the eminent American architectural historian, Henry-Russell Hitchcock, wrote:

> Glasgow in the last 150 years has had two of the greatest architects of the western world. Charles Rennie Mackintosh was not highly productive but his influence in Central Europe was comparable to such American architects as Louis Sullivan and Frank Lloyd Wright. An even greater and happily more productive architect, though one whose influence can only occasionally be traced in America in Milwaukee and in New York City and not as far as I know in Europe, was Alexander Thomson.

The reason for Thomson's comparatively modest influence was a simple one. It seems that he left Glasgow only once and, unlike Mackintosh, did not enter the world of international exhibitions and competitions. Instead, Alexander Thomson built up his architectural practice developing a unique design vocabulary that used ancient Greek, ancient Egyptian and Levantine sources. He became known as 'Greek Thomson', a nickname that did little justice to his range and talent.

In the villas he created in Langside, Pollokshields, Helensburgh and Cove, Thomson's imagination led him to design massive, horizontal houses rather than his soaring, monumental public buildings such as the Egyptian Halls in Union Street or the St Vincent Free Church. The classical frontages of the villas, with their columns and pediments retaining a pleasing formality and symmetry, do not overpower either their surroundings or their inhabitants. In what is known as the Prairie School of architecture (and this was one of the points Hitchcock was making), the likes of Frank Lloyd Wright were clearly influenced by Thomson's approach. Holmwood House in Cathcart is perhaps the finest example of his domestic work. It is both impressive – something the owner, a paper manufacturer, wanted – and homely, a place to raise a young family. Thomson designed many details, including the playful, colourful wall decorations, and laid out the garden. In 1999 the Clydesdale Bank issued a £20 note to mark Glasgow's designation as UK City of Architecture and Design, and it featured the dome of Holmwood and a portrait of Alexander Thomson.

In 1889 Charles Rennie Mackintosh joined the architectural practice of Honeyman and Keppie, and his career began to burgeon in prosperous Glasgow. In quick succession he designed the tower for the old *Glasgow Herald* building, Queen Margaret Medical College off Great Western Road (later occupied by the BBC), the Martyrs Public School in the Townhead, and, triumphantly, the new Glasgow School of Art in 1897. Its headmaster, Fra Newbery, was a tremendous supporter of Mackintosh and encouraged his innovative design. Newbery's daughter, Mary, knew Charles Rennie Mackintosh well and she gave an interview in 1985:

> When they saw the School of Art, it was too much – forty years ahead of its time. But that was the appearance of the Glasgow School of Art; inside it worked so well. It was a splendid working building. The people who objected or

couldn't swallow it, they didn't go inside to see what it was like. They just saw this curious castle-like place from Sauchiehall Street. It's still rather an odd building. Maybe a businessman wouldn't order a building like that. Even today when people look at the furniture and say how modern it is – not only that but the carpets, the lights – all look very suitable for today. They could have been designed yesterday . . .

If anyone else touched his work, he'd have literally torn them apart. While he was away once when the school was being built, Keppie, who was head of the firm, arranged for a cornice to be put in at the top, just above the stairs. Mackintosh didn't like cornices – he liked the walls to reach the ceiling – and when he came back he bounced with anger and fury and he had it all cut out . . . And there is still no cornice . . .

Thinking back now, I can see that the Glasgow School of Art alarmed people, and after the second phase, he never really got work. Le Corbusier did some very odd things in France but went on doing them. But Mackintosh didn't get the chance. He might have got more orthodox; you can't really tell. The Glasgow School of Art was so ahead of its time, he just had to wait for people to assimilate his ideas.

Despite the design of two beautiful houses, one in Helensburgh and the other in Kilmalcolm, Mackintosh was indeed never again commissioned to create a major building after the second phase of the School of Art in 1906. Before the outbreak of the First World War, he resigned from Honeyman and Keppie, and he and his wife moved to Walberswick in East Anglia where he painted watercolours. Then they moved to France. In 1928 Mackintosh died of cancer. Mary Newbery reflected:

> Looking back I feel terribly, terribly sad at the waste. Here we have this brilliant man it would pay you to use . . . Mackintosh could have designed anything, he just didn't get a chance. Perhaps he did all he was going to do, but I'd like to have seen his fiftieth house . . . with all the edges rubbed off and all his experience and development brought into play. We could have had somebody as good as Corbusier, but we weren't able to do it . . . Thinking back now, the tears come to my eyes and I feel so sad that the genius was wasted . . . I could weep at the waste of his genius.

In May 2014 the interior of the Glasgow School of Art was destroyed by a work of art. Flammable gas used in a student project was ignited by the heat of a projector and the building was quickly engulfed. Restoration began, but, astonishingly, another fire broke out in 2018. It was even more destructive than the first, gutting the building and badly damaging neighbouring premises. No conclusions have yet been reached about the cause of the second blaze, but it seems that the School of Art will not reopen until 2027 at the earliest and perhaps even as late as 2032. Known as 'The Mack' after its brilliant architect, the fate of this stunning building, perhaps Glasgow's greatest piece of architecture, is beyond sad.

19

Fitba

In the late summer of 1967 there was a serious road accident in Glasgow's city centre. It caused tremendous congestion, and as they did in those days, policemen and women walked back through the queues of stationary cars to inform motorists what had happened and tell them how long the delay might be. As a young policewoman approached a car, the passenger wound down his window. Furrowing her brow, she asked, 'Do I know you?' The passenger replied, 'Fitba, hen. Fitba.'

He was Jock Stein, the manager of Celtic Football Club. Earlier that summer, on 25 May in Lisbon, his team had won the European Cup. Not only were Celtic the first British team to do that, they were also the first in Northern Europe. Having won the Scottish League, the Scottish Cup, the Scottish League Cup and the Glasgow Cup, Celtic travelled to Portugal with high hopes. But they were not favourites to win. Their opposition was Inter Milan, the Italian team that had already won the European Cup in 1964 and 1965, and they also had a defensive system, the *catenaccio*, the door-bolt, that made it very difficult for teams to score against them. But before the match, Jock Stein was confident: "Celtic will be the first team to bring the European Cup back to Britain . . . we are going to attack as we have never attacked before."

Almost immediately, Stein's confidence looked misplaced. After only seven minutes, Inter Milan scored from a penalty and then retreated behind the *catenaccio*. This defensive set-up saw a back line of at least three or four players with a *libero*, a sweeper playing behind them to deal with any attacking player who broke through. And for the whole of the rest of the first half, it worked. Despite several near-misses hitting the crossbar of the goals more than once, Inter Milan's defence looked impregnable. Billy McNeill, the Celtic captain, later commented: 'Sometimes they had nine defenders back and only one player upfield.' But early in the second half, there was a spectacular breakthrough. The Celtic full-back Tommy Gemmell scored with a perfectly hit rocket from twenty-five yards. And a few minutes from full-time, Steve Chalmers scored the winning goal. Many Celtic fans had travelled to Portugal, and at the final whistle they invaded the pitch, delirious at the success of their heroes. Six of the players ran away from them, racing towards their own goal. Before kick-off, they had left their false teeth in Ronnie Simpson's goalkeeping hat at the back of the net and knowing there would be photographs, they needed to be able to smile. Celtic's achievement was also seen as a win for football, for their attacking play rather than the boring, defence-minded approach of Inter Milan.

It was an occasion for immense pride, a pride of lions, and the team became known as 'the Lisbon Lions'. They were all born and raised within a thirty-mile radius of Glasgow, and the European Cup was seen as a victory for the whole city, and for Scotland. The famous Liverpool manager, Bill Shankly, said to Jock Stein, 'You're immortal now.' He may have been, but he was still unrecognisable to a young Glasgow policewoman.

Rangers also achieved European glory when they won the Cup Winners Cup in 1972, beating Dynamo Moscow 3–2 in

Barcelona. It was the completion of another circle of footballing history for the city, for exactly 100 years earlier, Glasgow had seen the beginnings of international matches. On 30 November 1872, at the West of Scotland cricket ground in Partick, Scotland played England. This, the first football international to be played anywhere, was watched by 4,000 spectators and ended in a 0–0 draw.

The match was arranged by Queen's Park FC. The club was founded in 1867, the oldest in Scotland. Taking its name from the district of Glasgow where it played, in the Southside, its players and officials dominated the game for much of the later nineteenth century. The team even played in the FA Cup in England, only to lose twice in the final. In 1873 Queen's Park formed the Scottish Football Association with eight other clubs: Kilmarnock, Clydesdale, Vale of Leven, Dumbreck, Third Lanark, Eastern and Granville. Only Queen's Park and Kilmarnock have survived into the modern era. The year before, the Secretary of the (English) Football Association, Charles Alcock, had issued a challenge that invited a Scotland team to play against England. Since it was not clear whom exactly he was challenging – there being no Scottish Football Association at that time – Queen's Park stepped up. On St Andrew's Day, 30 November, at the West of Scotland Cricket Club ground in Partick, the entire Scotland team was made up of Queen's Park players, and because those were the club colours at the time, they played in dark blue, a strip adopted by many Scottish sports for their international teams.

It had rained for three days before the match, and that had been inhibiting for the Glasgow team. They had perfected a different approach to football. Up until that point, the game was about dribbling, individual players keeping the ball to themselves and trying to get past or around the opposition to score. Queen's Park had begun to play the game by advancing up the field by passing the ball between different players, but it may be that the wet weather had hampered their style. The final score was a goalless draw. What might also have been influential was an early version of the *catenaccio*. Apparently England played with eight forwards, and that allowed them to work an effective offside trap. At one point, the England goalkeeper, Robert Barker of Hertfordshire Rangers, switched places with a forward, William Maynard. Perhaps he was bored.

After the first international match in 1872, larger stadia were built to accommodate ever-increasing crowds. Hampden Park was named for the prosaic and surprising reason that it was near Hampden Terrace, in the Mount Florida district of the city. The street had been named after John Hampden, a noted soldier in the parliament forces during the War of the Three Kingdoms (often miscalled the English Civil War). Queen's Park's new ground opened in 1903 with a capacity of 100,000. Glasgow now has four professional football clubs with Partick Thistle (founded in 1876, they play in Maryhill, nowhere near Partick) joining Queen's Park and Celtic and Rangers.

20

Glasgow Fly Men

The city's reputation as a builder of ships and the manufacturer of railway locomotives is solid and well known. Much less attention has been paid to Glasgow's attempts to get an aviation industry off the ground. Which is a great shame, because, if anything, the inventiveness of the city's fly men was remarkable, even sometimes heroic.

In 1905 Edwin Mumford of William Denny & Brothers, a shipbuilder based at Dumbarton, designed and built a prototype helicopter, what he called a 'direct-lift air-craft'. Six 'lifting screws' shaped more like ships' propellers and made from fabric stretched over wooden frames were intended to get the aircraft airborne. They looked elegant, like a series of huge ladies' fans, but they were very fragile. The first prototype needed to be as light as possible because it was driven by a small (only forty-horsepower), four-cylinder, two-stroke engine. And so Mumford had the fuselage made from bamboo. But it was found to absorb water too readily, making the aircraft too heavy to fly. It was destroyed in a storm in 1909.

A new version was built with an aluminium frame and test flights were carried out between 1912 and 1914, with floats attached to the undercarriage rather than wheels. The little direct-lift aircraft was towed out into the Clyde, where it made a successful 'hop' of about a hundred yards at a height of ten feet. Edwin Mumford's basic problem was that he could never get enough power from the small engines that were available. When war broke out in 1914, he abandoned the project and went back to shipbuilding.

During the First World War, George Weir of G. & J. Weir (now the Weir Group) had been the government's director general of aircraft production, and after 1918 he and his brother James became fascinated by 'autogiros'. Based in Cathcart, Weir's had manufactured aero engines and aircraft, turning out 1,100 by the close of hostilities, many of them the FE2 biplane fighter and bomber. But the brothers believed the future lay elsewhere. In 1926 they backed the Cierva Autogiro Company to develop the designs of Juan de la Cierva, a Spanish pilot and engineer. His autogiros looked (and in fact were) a cross between a light aeroplane with short, narrow wings to give it stability and a helicopter-style rotor above the fuselage. These little aircraft could not fly vertically, but they needed only a very short runway to take off and land. Which gave them great versatility and flexibility. But, in 1936, Juan de la Cierva was killed in an air accident in Croydon. Nevertheless, the company carried on, and by 1948 it had produced the Cierva Air Horse, up until that time the largest helicopter yet built.

During the First World War William Beardmore & Co., owner of the great Parkhead Forge in Glasgow's East End, became heavily involved in aircraft production, building the famous Sopwith Pup fighter at Dalmuir on the lower Clyde. Sir William's company had also made a succession of huge rigid airships, including the successful R34, which had completed the first-ever return transatlantic flight. But tragedy was to follow when the R101 went down in flames on its maiden international flight to France, killing forty-eight people. The accident effectively brought airship production to an end.

In 1925 Beardmore began building one of the largest aeroplanes the world had ever seen. Dubbed 'The Inflexible', it had an enormous wingspan of 157 feet, stood 21 feet high, had a wing area of almost 2,000 square feet and wheels that were seven feet in diameter. Powered by three Roll-Royce Condor engines (one mounted on each of the wings and the third on the nose), 'The Inflexible' had a maximum speed of 110 miles an hour and could fly as high as 9,000 feet.

This gigantic aircraft was built in sections at Dalmuir, shipped down to Folkestone and transported by road to the Aeroplane and Armament Experimental Establishment at Martlesham Heath in Suffolk, where it was assembled. The aeroplane first flew on 5 March 1928, and when a reporter from the influential magazine *Flight* saw it, he wrote that: 'We may have our doubts as to the efficiency of a very large aeroplane, but in spite of ourselves, we are impressed.' He added that 'The Inflexible' had flown well and proved to be controllable, but it had also been nicknamed 'The Incredible' and 'The Impossible'.

Sir William Beardmore had visions of large aircraft such as his flying passengers around the world. But, sadly, his notorious financial recklessness had undermined the company, and by the late 1930s it had collapsed. And so Glasgow's Fly Men were never able to establish an aviation industry in the city. But it was not for the want of trying or a lack of imagination.

21

The Clockwork Orange

One distinguished journalist reckons that it was Sir Peter Parker, the chairman of British Rail from 1976 to 1983, who coined the nickname for the Glasgow Underground. While surveying the new carriages, officially painted 'Strathclyde Red' but actually a bright orange, he is reputed to have remarked: 'So these are the original Clockwork Orange.' Much more likely is that the nickname is a popular Glaswegian perception, an example of citizens enjoying a good joke. The circular line perhaps reminds people of model trains going round and round in a circle on the sitting-room carpet, and before recent refurbishment the trains and coaches were a wee bit shoogly and often broke down.

In fact, the Glasgow Underground was, just as much as all the industry along the banks of the Clyde, a persuasive symbol of the city's status as the Second City of the Empire. When it opened in 1896, the line was the fourth oldest on the planet, the first being London (1863), the second, Istanbul (1875) and third, Budapest (1896). Even now, only Newcastle and Liverpool have underground rail systems. Birmingham doesn't, and, more to the point, neither does Edinburgh. All they've got is a single 14km tramway that was five years late and £400 million over budget.

In 1891 the Glasgow District Subway Company began digging the necessary tunnels, and five years later the route was complete. It was designed as a loop formed by two lines, one carrying trains travelling clockwise and the other anti-clockwise. More evidence for a Glasgow origin for the nickname. Trains were hauled by a steam-powered system of cables along tracks that were only four feet wide, a feature that may have contributed to the shoogliness. Wooden-bodied coaches were built in Motherwell and a firm in Worcestershire, and island platforms to serve both the clockwise and anti-clockwise trains were constructed at all fifteen stations.

On the December day when the new railway opened, the service did not start well. Two carriages carrying sixty passengers banged into one another in the tunnel under the Clyde. Four people were injured, one person had to be carted off to the Royal Infirmary to be patched up, and the rest probably thought twice about using this new mode of transport around the city. Maybe trams were better.

In 1923 the underground was bought by Glasgow Corporation for £385,000. The cable-hauling system remained in place until 1935 when the city had to fork out another £120,000 to electrify the lines. When the Second World War broke out four years later, the carriages were packed with the workers who poured through the gates of the shipyards and the munitions and armament factories on the Clyde. But, unlike London, the underground was never used as a bomb shelter because, apart from those under the Clyde, the tunnels were not deep enough. Only one German bomb came anywhere near when it fell on Merkland Street Station (now closed) and it did enough damage to close that section of the line.

Much more damage was done by Dr Richard Beeching in the 1960s when he overhauled, and then closed down, much of Britain's rail transport infrastructure. Both the St Enoch and Buchanan Street mainline stations went out of use, and that created an unfortunate disjunction. London's Underground system links all the city's railway stations, which makes for much faster commuting and keeps people and traffic off the streets for longer. Despite protests, the Beeching axe fell and both of the Glasgow stations were demolished.

By that time, the Clockwork Orange was in a bad way. The stations were rundown, there were no escalators, the ticket offices were old-fashioned and slow, the carriages smelly, even more shoogly, and in those days smoking was allowed. Trains often broke down, and the maintenance engineers were overwhelmed. In the early 1970s the Greater Glasgow Passenger Transport Executive took over, and in 1974 it announced that the system would close for three years so that it could be modernised.

Much smartened up and shiny, the refurbished system was reopened by Queen Elizabeth II in November 1979. Since then, new carriages (designed at the Glasgow School of Art) have been brought into service with a new livery, new staff uniforms, new gates to the stations and new ticketing systems. All stations were rebuilt and enlarged, and included new features such as escalators. Best of all, new trains have made the line faster and more reliable. The carriages are painted white with orange panels on the doors.

The underground now carries around 13 million passengers a year and is run by the Strathclyde Partnership for Transport. Trains run every four minutes at peak times, but running times are modest – 6.30 a.m. to 11.40 p.m. on weekdays and 10 a.m. to 6.12 p.m. on Sundays. This has nothing to do with Glasgow's religious sensibilities. Sunday evening is when the trains are cleaned, serviced and repaired. Villains, vandals and graffiti artists are kept in check not by the Glasgow polis but by the British Transport Police.

The Clockwork Orange has come a long way since 1896. But somehow it has contrived to change a great deal while staying much the same. The rail gauge of only four feet and the tunnel diameter of eleven feet are what they always were. And while the Swiss-built carriages run like clockwork, as they should, they are just as shoogly as the old ones.

22

The Collectors

Late on a summer afternoon in 1950, a vacuum cleaner salesman took a chance. On his way back from Berwick to Duns, he drove through an imposing gateway and up a long drive to a castle. After a bad day with no sales, he thought he had nothing to lose and surely anyone who lived in a castle would be able to afford a new hoover. When the salesman parked, there seemed to be no one about, but when he pulled at the bell, it clanged loudly inside. The huge oak door was swung open by a tall, cadaverous man in a three-piece suit.

'No, thank you,' he said, and then hesitated. 'Look,' he went on, 'I'm doing nothing. Would you like to have a look around?'

The owner of Hutton Castle in Berwickshire was Britain's greatest private art collector, the former Glasgow shipping magnate, Sir William Burrell. The salesman remembered two suits of armour on either side of the front door, a series of vast rooms, most of them hung with tapestries, many with exquisite pieces of sculpture, some with ancient stained-glass panels set into big windows to catch the light, all stuffed with works of art of all kinds. In particular, he was struck by the number of Persian and Turkish carpets piled up on top of each other in the outhouses and garage.

'There were beautiful things everywhere – paintings, china and all sorts. It was all beautiful, and Sir William knew his stuff, telling me where everything came from. But I felt it was an obsession, the collection, like an itch he couldn't scratch . . . I couldn't persuade him he needed another vacuum cleaner though.'

Born in Glasgow in 1861, William began work in the family firm when he was fourteen. Burrell & Son were ship owners, one of the leading cargo carriers in Britain, and the young man quickly showed a flair for business. He began to compile a sizeable fortune, and with the outbreak of the First World War, made even more money by selling most of his ships for far more than he had paid. Like many successful entrepreneurs, he took risks, buying at the bottom of the market, hoping it would rise. And in 1914, it did, spectacularly.

William Burrell also had a flair for art collecting. He began to acquire tapestries, stained glass and furniture. By 1944 his collection ran to a staggering 6,000 items valued at approximately £1 million. Burrell and his wife, Constance, decided to donate it all to their native city of Glasgow, and also added £450,000 in cash so that a gallery could be built to show it to the public. Unlike many acquisitive private collectors, he wanted others to derive as much pleasure from beautiful objects as he did. That was why Burrell showed the salesman around Hutton Castle. But he attached conditions to his gift to the city: the gallery had to be built within four miles of Killearn and not less than sixteen miles from Glasgow Royal Exchange. It was not until the Corporation acquired Pollok Country Park in 1967 that a compliant and suitable site became available. Even then, it took a long time coming. The stunning building that houses the Burrell Collection, brilliantly conceived and designed by Barry Gasson, was opened by the late Queen in 1983. With its soaring spaces, intimate corners and the lovely, glass-walled woodland gallery, it is a fitting setting for a remarkable collection. The ship owner's act of philanthropy was rightly described as 'one of the greatest gifts ever made to any city in the world'.

Sir William Burrell was by no means unique. Glasgow had an established tradition of wealthy men who collected art, mostly as a signifier of status and often as an investment. War was the stimulus for its beginnings. After the seismic and ruinous upheavals of the Napoleonic Wars, one art dealer from Glasgow was very active. Preferring to describe himself as 'a speculator', William Buchanan documented his activities in the ponderously titled *Memoirs of Painting, with a Chronological History of the Importation of Pictures by the Great Masters into England since the French Revolution*. Published in 1824, it listed a great number of works, some of which eventually made their way to Glasgow. The collections of fallen French aristocrats like Charles-Maurice de Talleyrand-Périgord were bought very cheaply from desperate or ignorant sellers by Buchanan and his agents, and they kept cash-rich British collectors well supplied. The great Orléans Sale was the disposal of the collection of Philippe II, duc d'Orléans, and much of it passed through Buchanan's hands on its way across the Channel.

William Buchanan was not averse to underhand tactics to complete a lucrative sale. Paintings by lesser artists were attributed to more famous names of the same place and period, and his network of agents offered bribes both to sellers and to the advisors of prospective buyers. But William did one dodgy deal too many and died in bankruptcy in 1864 in his brother's house in Blythswood Square.

The late eighteenth-century painter and art dealer Gavin Hamilton was of a very different stamp, but also influential in bringing the great art of Europe to his native Glasgow. Having gone to live in Italy, Hamilton became interested in archaeology. After excavating Emperor Hadrian's villa at Tivoli, near

Rome, he had the sculpture he found shipped to Britain. The great Warwick Vase, one of the featured pieces in the Burrell Collection, was found in fragments by Hamilton and his men, in a marshy pond in the villa's grounds, in 1771. Hamilton had the knowledge and the wit to understand what they had found. Only a few new pieces of marble had to be used to fit it all back together. Around its rim are wonderfully detailed sculptured heads linked to the cult of the god Bacchus.

As Glasgow's economy boomed and great profits were made in the second half of the nineteenth century, more and more successful businessmen became collectors – and rivals. As well as William Burrell, Archibald McLellan (whose galleries still stand in Sauchiehall Street), T. G. Arthur, Thomas Carmichael and W. A. Coats of the famous threadmaking company based in Paisley all compiled extensive collections. Arthur Kay specialised in acquiring Dutch Old Masters and Japanese lacquer work. In 1892 he took a risk when he bought paintings by the controversial French Impressionists Degas, Manet and Monet. Kay gifted several works to Glasgow's public galleries. The city's collection of collections is outstanding. The Kelvingrove Art Gallery and Museum, the Museum of Modern Art, the Hunterian, the People's Palace and of course the Burrell Collection were hugely enriched by gifts from the estates of these wealthy men, who not only bought great art, but also had a sense of civic duty and pride in their native city. Outside London, there is nowhere in Britain with a more impressive and wide-ranging, world-class array of municipal art accessible to all.

23

The Glasgow Boys and Girls

Where there are wealthy individuals who wish to buy art, there are usually dealers who act as middle-men, who have relationships with painters, sculptors and other artists. W. Craibe Angus was one of the most influential. He knew the painter James McNeill Whistler very well and was often in a position to sell on his work and take a commission for doing so. In 1881, Angus sold Whistler's *Arrangement in Black and Brown: The Fur Jacket* to William Burrell for £400 and he took £60 in commission for arranging the sale. The dealer also kept artists informed of trends, of what the customer might want to buy, and sometimes they took the initiative. Whistler offered W. Craibe Angus his *Nocturne in Blue and Gold: Southampton Water* for 130 guineas and suggested that he could sell it on for £200. It was a business, like any other.

Encouraged by the early dealers like William Buchanan, collectors tended to look to Europe for safe investments in art, but they also offered opportunity to local painters. A group of (mainly) young men began to look differently at landscape painting in particular, and instead of the classical, idealised, heavily varnished work of Europeans, what they called 'glue-pot' art, they developed a much more realistic eye. Rather than depicting romantic Highland scenery or famous moments in Scotland's history, they preferred the everyday realities of rural life. Farm labourers at work in the fields, a young lass cutting cabbages, another driving geese, a carpenter up to his knees in wood shavings.

This group of artists became known as the Glasgow Boys. There were originally seven of them, all friends or friends of friends: James Guthrie, George Henry, John Lavery, James Paterson, Edward A. Walton, Joseph Crawhall and William York MacGregor. Sometimes they worked together in MacGregor's studio in Bath Street, but they spent much of the spring, summer and autumn in the countryside, painting out of doors, often in East Lothian and Kirkcudbrightshire. These seven were the core, but others came and went. They would paint alongside the Glasgow Boys, no doubt exchanging ideas and opinions before going their separate ways. There are approximately twenty painters associated with the group. By far the most influential was one whose name has been largely forgotten. Arthur Melville eventually tired of working in Scotland and migrated to the Mediterranean, where he painted vivid landscapes and rural scenes full of light and colour.

In 1888 Glasgow decided to advertise itself and its achievements on an international stage. In Kelvingrove Park, between May and November, the city mounted the International Exhibition of Science, Art and Industry. Its unblushing aim was to draw attention to Glasgow's initiatives in engineering, industry and the arts in the second half of the nineteenth century. The hope was also that the great exhibition would raise enough money to build a municipal museum and art gallery. It was also the making of the Glasgow Boys. Local artists rather than those from Europe or England were featured, and four exhibited their work: John Lavery, George Henry, Edward A. Walton and James Guthrie. Lavery was appointed artist-in-residence at the exhibition. And it worked. In 1890 the Glasgow Boys were exhibited at the Grosvenor

Gallery in Bond Street in London. The national press went into raptures about their work and it was taken up in Europe when the Munich International Exhibition showed their output. At the request of the great impresario Sergei Diaghilev, some of their paintings were shown in St Petersburg.

As the Boys were celebrating, a group of Glasgow Girls were hard at work. These artists are often forgotten or under-represented. Margaret MacDonald, wife of Charles Rennie Mackintosh, was a substantial artist in her own right. She painted and created magnificent gesso panels for the interiors of her husband's designs. With her sister, Frances, and brother-in-law, Herbert McNair, they became 'The Four', working together on textile designs, metalwork, graphics and book illustrations. Frances and Margaret MacDonald exhibited their work in London, Liverpool and Venice. Glasgow being Glasgow, they became known as 'The Spook School', a reference to their more otherworldly output.

Perhaps the greatest of the Glasgow Girls was also one of the shortest-lived. Bessie MacNicol died in 1904, only thirty-five years old, but she worked hard in her all too brief career. Like several of the Glasgow Boys, she was drawn to Galloway and Kirkcudbright in particular. Her portraits are very striking, and the painting of Hornel in his studio is especially atmospheric, drawing in those who look at it. Against a highly coloured background, Hornel wears a black jacket while holding his palette and a fistful of brushes. But it is his eyes that are magnetic, a painter's eyes.

Light was what persuaded the Glasgow Boys and Girls to go down to Kirkcudbright, Galloway and elsewhere in rural Scotland. Its landscape was different, and perhaps these qualities were best explained by a later Glasgow Girl, one of the greatest painters Scotland has ever seen. Having graduated from the Glasgow School of Art in 1947 with a postgraduate diploma, Joan Eardley began to work in the Townhead district of the city, renting and setting up a studio. Her portraits of local children in what was a very poor, overcrowded, inner-city slum were particularly powerful and memorable. But, in 1950, she sought a very different source of inspiration. Eardley travelled to Catterline, a tiny fishing village south of Stonehaven. In a BBC radio interview, Eardley offered something that sounds like a manifesto, certainly an explanation of where all her visceral power as a painter came from:

> Catterline has such a terrific clarity and terrific light, whereas Glasgow feels as though it has a sort of lid on top of it, but at the same time it's [Catterline] a little community, and the place I chose to paint in Glasgow is also a little community in a certain district, a little back street, where everybody knew everybody else. The same thing seems to be the case in the village where I live in the north-east. It's the sort of intimate thing I like, and I think you've got to know something before you paint it . . . I suppose I'm essentially a romantic. I believe in the sort of emotion that you get from what your eyes show you and what you feel about certain things. Well, I don't really know what I'm painting, I'm just trying to paint.

24

Glasgow at War: the Home Front

As a series of diplomatic misunderstandings, mobilisations and political blunders followed each other, war clouds gathered over Europe in the late summer of 1914, and in August Great Britain and its Empire went to war with Germany, Austria and Turkey. The reasons for the conflict were never easy to grasp, then and now, but in the Second City of the Empire few men hesitated when Field Marshal Lord Kitchener pointed at them from the iconic poster. Even though it was far from clear why their country needed them, Glasgow's instinctive patriotism was such that thousands of men volunteered to join the armed forces. It has been estimated that the city and its immediate environs sent more than 200,000 volunteers and conscripts into battle. This spasm of enthusiasm caused problems. Out of a force only 2,000 strong, 386 Glasgow policemen and 45 members of the fire brigade answered Kitchener's call. The city's firemaster complained to the British government, and firemen were immediately exempted from conscription.

Most men served in famous West of Scotland regiments such as the Highland Light Infantry, the Cameronians and the Argyll and Sutherland Highlanders, and there were Glaswegians in almost every regiment in the British army, and in the Royal Navy and the Merchant Marine. One of the most ardent recruiters was Donald MacAlister, the principal of Glasgow University. He had personal reasons. When war was declared, MacAlister had been in Germany and was detained for a short time. On his return, he was eager to fight against his captors and all 400 students in the university's Officer Training Corps enlisted. Since the casualty rate amongst junior officers was very high, as they led their men 'over the top' in the trenches in Flanders, many were killed. Nineteen from the university died at Passchendaele alone.

Because of Glasgow's history of poor housing conditions and insufficient nutrition, many of the newly enlisted Glaswegians fell below the British Army's minimum height of five foot five inches. These men joined special 'bantam' battalions to form the Bantam Division, the 35th Infantry Division. They proved themselves again and again in combat.

After it became clear that it would not be all over by Christmas, and that the German Army were well organised and determined, Glasgow's industry adapted swiftly to the needs of a longer war. Shipyards, toolmakers, steel workers and coal mines all increased production while other factories converted to the manufacture of munitions. Six of the yards on the Clyde became crucial to the war effort: John Brown & Company of Clydebank, Fairfield of Govan, Beardmore of Dalmuir, Scott's of Greenock, Denny's of Dumbarton and Yarrow's of Scotstoun. Together they turned out more than 250 ships: battleships, cruisers, early versions of aircraft carriers, submarines, gunboats, depot ships and dozens of fast, well-armed destroyers. Britain's strategy was to blockade the German Navy, not allow them out of the North Sea, so that Germany would slowly be starved into surrender.

Other yards worked at full capacity to produce the essential merchant ships Britain needed to keep itself supplied and to replace those that had been sunk by German submarines. The most notorious casualty was the ocean liner, the *Lusitania*, built on the Clyde. It sank with the loss of 1,198 off the Irish coast in 1915.

To supply the vast quantities of steel needed for all that production, the Ministry of Munitions paid for the upgrade of some of the ageing steel works in North Lanarkshire. Some needed their furnaces to be completely rebuilt. In turn, the coal mines were required to increase their output. This had a knock-on effect that spilled over into conflict. Skilled workers and labourers flocked to Glasgow to work in these expanding factories and yards, and that put pressure on housing. Most of the city's stock was in private hands, and landlords took the opportunity to put up rents. In 1915 there was a series of rent strikes, many of them led by women, some of whose husbands were in the armed forces. They saw their landlords as an enemy worse than the Germans. 'We Are Fighting the Huns at Home' read one placard. Another had 'Fighting Prussians in Partick'. The anger at the profiteering and injustice was spreading to the workers in the shipyards, and the government was forced to intervene and freeze all rents at pre-war levels. It was a major, early victory for female activism.

At one end of the political spectrum, the Glasgow rent strikes were seen as an important stage in the struggles of ordinary people, the beginnings of socialism. Others saw it as the start of what became known as 'Red Clydeside', a reputation that has arguably done Glasgow some harm by scaring away investors in the light industries that flourished elsewhere after the war.

There was also another, perhaps more important, impact. As more and more men joined the armed forces, women were employed to produce the shells, bombs, ammunition and grenades needed. This hastened the time when women were granted the right to vote, and it encouraged others to take part in political activism. Mary Bell was one of a group of five pioneering women elected as councillors to Glasgow Corporation in 1920. She later became a baillie, a magistrate, and in that capacity was required to witness the execution of John Keen, convicted for murder. 'Many people urged me not to attend the execution,' Bell later wrote, 'but I wanted to prove that a woman is fit to take her place on the public bodies. We women in the civic body of a city like Glasgow are pioneers of the women's movement, and we need to show that we are fit to take the unpleasant with the pleasant.'

Life could be very unpleasant for German nationals living in an around Glasgow in 1914 and afterwards. Many Germans, Austrians and Turks were rounded up and interned on the Isle of Man. To begin with, they were treated firmly but reasonably, but after the sinking of the *Lusitania*, the mood darkened. There were anti-German riots in Liverpool, Manchester and London, but not in Glasgow. In Greenock, a German ladies' hair salon had its window broken.

There is no doubt that the First World War had major effects on the city of Glasgow. The first and most obvious was the scale of the slaughter. Glaswegians locked in the grinding, blood-soaked struggle in the trenches in Flanders paid a terrible price. The casualty rate was huge. One historian reckons that out of 557,000 Scots in the armed forces, more than 147,200 were killed. It was a mortality rate of 26 per cent. The lists of the fallen on war memorials all over the city are very long. Many also suffered life-changing injury, while the health of others, especially those who had been gassed, never recovered. A citizen army would never submit to such slaughter again.

The war also shook up the working practices of the shipyards, the engineering firms and other manufacturers as unions began to become more powerful. The politics of Glasgow changed and gave the Clyde a troublesome reputation it did not deserve, but also speeded the birth of the modern Labour Party. The war and its aftermath gave voice to a number of men who were to loom large in the post-war period. Among them were David Kirkwood, Patrick Dollan, John Maclean, Willie Gallacher, James Maxton and John Wheatley.

25

Glasgow at War: the Front

On a misty, late winter morning in 1922, crowds gathered outside Glasgow Cathedral. Led by two officers wearing full decorations, a colour party carried six flags and many men saluted as they passed and entered the great church. The colours of the 15th, 16th and 17th Battalions of the Highland Light Infantry were being installed in places of honour. Raised in 1914 in response to Lord Kitchener's appeal, these volunteers were originally known as the 1st, 2nd and 3rd Glasgow Battalions. And because many of the men knew each other, they were also known as Pals Battalions, something encouraged by the War Office since old soldiers like Kitchener knew that while men do fight for their country, they also fight for each other. Nicknames remembered the origins of these recruits. For some reason now obscure, the 15th were known as 'the Boozy Boys' despite being officially labelled as the Glasgow Tramways Battalion since most had worked on the city's tram service.

Set to the First World War anthem, 'It's A Long Way To Tipperary', there exists poignant film footage of these men marching in their green tram services uniforms through the streets of Glasgow to what might be George Square. So many had volunteered that the British army had run out of uniforms. Many men smiled as they passed the camera. And many of them would never see Glasgow again. Once the marching column had come to a halt, a group of civic dignitaries appeared in order to review them. One wore a top hat and a chain of office, Lord Provost Sir Daniel Macauley Stevenson.

The 16th Battalion of the Highland Light Infantry were known as 'the Holy Second' because most of the original recruits were from the Glasgow battalion of the Boys' Brigade. Two years after they volunteered and marched through the city, some of them would find themselves stranded in the landscape of hell.

After a storm destroyed the tents of their training camp at the appropriately named village of Gailes in Ayrshire, the 17th Battalion of the Highland Light Infantry was moved to comfortable billets in the Clyde holiday resort of Troon. They immediately became known as 'the Featherbeds'. Their original designation was as 'the Glasgow Chamber of Commerce Battalion', and most of their recruits were students at the Royal Glasgow Technical College (the direct predecessor of Strathclyde University) or former pupils of the private schools, Glasgow Academy and Glasgow High School. Others were white-collar workers in local businesses. When they arrived in France, those comparatively comfortable origins would seem very distant.

Although there were several important other theatres of conflict, especially in Eastern Europe, the focus of the First World War was in Flanders, the border region between Belgium and France. The grinding, attritional struggle in the trenches was tremendously destructive as artillery reduced the landscape to flattened, pock-marked ruins, punctuated only by the trunks of broken, blasted, blackened trees and the rubble of villages and towns. The war was static, and the same places were pounded again and again. And everywhere there was death. Millions of men were blown to smithereens or brutally injured by shells and mines, or were cut to pieces in futile, 'over the top' charges as machine-gun fire ripped through them. Perhaps the most destructive phase of this terrible war was the Battle of the Somme in 1916. At a cost of more than a million casualties on both sides, only six miles of territory was gained by the British and French.

In the final days of the battle, the 16th Battalion of the Highland Light Infantry (the Boys' Brigade recruits from Glasgow) advanced at the village of Beaumont-Hamel, north-east of the city of Amiens. They broke through and occupied a German position, the Frankfurt Trench. But as the enemy counterattacked, 130 men of the 16th found that they were stranded, surrounded by German troops and left behind more than 800 yards north of British lines. Led by Company Sergeant-Major George Lee, a former Glasgow Corporation roads man, and Lance-Corporal John Veitch, a compositor in the printing trade from Anderston, they held out against overwhelming odds, attacked on all sides. Certain that the British commanders who led the retreat will have assumed they were all killed or wounded and captured, Lee sent two runners through the German lines. They probably evaded detection in the darkness because it was cold and snowing and most German soldiers were trying to keep warm. But subsequent British efforts to reach the stranded men all failed.

Despite the fact that they had very little food and no fresh water (soldiers crawled out of the trench to collect snowmelt from shell holes), Lee, Veitch and the former BBs from Glasgow held out for seven days as the Germans repeatedly shelled and attacked the Frankfurt Trench. There was hand-to-hand fighting, and both Lee and Veitch were killed. On the seventh day of the siege, the German commander offered to accept an honourable surrender, but the survivors declined and decided to fight on through the sleet and the snow.

When the Germans finally overwhelmed the trench the day after, they found only fifteen men able to hold a rifle and all of the other defenders either dead or wounded. When a baffled German officer saw the bedraggled, starving Glaswegians, he said, 'Is this what has held up my brigade for a week?' George Lee and John Veitch were recommended for posthumous Victoria Crosses, one survivor was awarded the Distinguished Service Order, there were two Military Crosses, eleven Distinguished Conduct Medals and twenty-two Military Medals for this extraordinary group of Glaswegians. The courage of the baggage handler John Smeaton and the others who attacked the terrorists at Glasgow Airport was only part of a long tradition.

There is a magnificent memorial to the 51st Highland Division of a kilted soldier at Beaumont-Hamel, and close by, some of the trenches and shell holes have been left as they were as a reminder of what happened to the fertile farmland of Flanders more than a hundred years ago. The distance between British and German trenches is surprisingly short. Not far away, another memorial is also very poignant. From 192 stones gathered from the battlefield at Culloden, one for every Scottish soldier killed in that small area, there is a cairn. On top sits a cobblestone from a Glasgow street. The height of the cairn is five feet and seven inches, the minimum stature required for recruits to the Highland Light Infantry – except for the Glasgow Bantams. And below a plaque commemorating the bravery of all these men is another smaller inscription: *Ici fleurira toujours le glorieux chardon d'Ecosse parmi les coquelicots de France.*

The glorious Scottish thistle will always flower here amongst the poppies of France.

26

You'll Have Had Your Tea

The Dough School was the result of a merger, or perhaps a mixture, of two earlier institutions to form the Glasgow and West of Scotland College of Domestic Sciences in 1910. Its nickname might be interpreted in two, or perhaps three, ways. Either it was a reference to the fact that young women were taught how to bake, or it was a diminutive of 'Domestic', or it was both. The college was established at Park Drive in the West End of the city, but was very soon afterwards converted into a hospital after the outbreak of the First World War. The Dough School was a response to the 1908 Education Act (Scotland) and its insistence on the provision of domestic education in schools – for girls. They needed teachers, and the college duly trained them.

This gender segregation continued well into the 1970s, when schoolgirls were still taught domestic science (later known as home economics) while boys attended metalwork and woodwork classes, or, occasionally technical drawing. The college had aspirations to help working-class women on low incomes make better use of scarce food resources, but these were generally unrealistic. During the First World War, the Dough School set up a canteen for servicemen in St Enoch's Square and served a staggering 1,537,000 meals. They also ran a mobile canteen.

In the 1930s a 'Bride's Course' was very popular. For a fee, young women who had become engaged could have twenty-four lessons in cookery practice, twelve in needlework, twelve in how to do laundry, twelve on home nursing, and if that went wrong, ten on first aid. In 1949 the college offered classes to women whose families were about to emigrate, telling them what to expect in the likes of Australia, New Zealand or Canada. And when, in the 1950s, the employment of domestic servants became a thing of the prewar past, middle-class women, who had perhaps omitted to sign up for the Bride's Course, had to learn skills their mothers did not need.

An enduring, useful, even iconic legacy of the Dough School is *The Glasgow Cookery Book*. Originally a textbook, one that was derived from notes and used in the school, it is very comprehensive and simple to use. More than 400 pages offer clear, brief and precise instructions on how to make everything from cheese puffs to vegetable marrow and apple chutney, on how to joint a chicken (with illustrations) and how to make pastry (also with illustrations). Sadly, some recipes have been removed. Government food safety legislation, for some benighted reason, does not allow the cooking of Sheep's Head Broth. What a waste. Despite this meddling, *The Glasgow Cookery Book* is a cultural adornment to the city and it has been continuously in print for more than a century. In 1995 the Dough School became part of Glasgow Caledonian University.

Its famous cookery book does not, sadly, contain a recipe for Glasgow's best known, most widely enjoyed, culinary product, what might be considered Britain's national dish. In 2009 the MP Mohammad Sarwar petitioned the European Union for the city to be given Protected Designation of Origin status for chicken tikka masala. The recipe owes its creation to the improvising skills of Ali Ahmed Aslam, the proprietor of the Shish Mahal restaurant that used to be in

Gibson Street in the West End. Using spices marinaded in the contents of a tin of condensed tomato soup, he created the famous sauce for a customer who had complained his meal was too dry. Mohammad Sarwar wanted the dish to be given the same protection as other uniquely Scottish food such as Arbroath smokies. He added: 'Glasgow's contribution to popular cuisine deserves to be more widely recognised . . . Glaswegians love the flavour of Asian spices but still want a bit of gravy on their meat. The Shish Mahal pioneered great Asian food with a Glasgow twist.' Despite the backing of Glasgow City Council, the application was not successful.

In 2014 Glasgow hosted the Commonwealth Games, and at the opening ceremony dancers appeared in costumes based on Tunnock's teacakes. They were followed by versions of the Loch Ness Monster, a Highland cow, a Highland pony and Dolly the Sheep. Every one a Scottish icon. Tunnock's is based at Uddingston, southeast of the city centre, and its two most famous and most loved products are the chocolate-coated marshmallow (on a biscuit base) teacakes and their caramel wafers. Both are glorious, distinctive and more-ish. In the 1960s RAF bomber crews were especially fond of the teacakes and never flew without them. Apparently, they expand at high altitude, but after one was left unwrapped (and, mystifyingly, not immediately eaten) and exploded on the instrument panel, they were banned. (In April 2025 the teacakes were given the official all-clear to fly again after the RAF Centre of Aerospace Medicine conducted some rigorous altitude experiments.) While Tunnock's teacakes are soft and creamy, the caramel wafers are crisp, and do not explode but deliciously disintegrate in the mouth. They consist of five layers of wafer and four of caramel, a perfect proportion. For forty-four years, the University of St Andrews was home to the Tunnock's Caramel Wafer Appreciation Society.

There can be no statistical doubt that all of these culinary delights from Glasgow have been washed down by another famous product made near the city. Barr's Irn-Bru, Scotland's other national drink, is its most popular soft drink, making the country unique in not preferring Coca-Cola. It was originally made in Parkhead, but production moved to Cumbernauld in 2000. Invented in 1901 by A. G. Barr, it was known as Iron Brew until 1946. More daft government legislation insisted that the product marketing should be 'literally true', and since the drink was not brewed and not made from iron, it became Irn-Bru. Mercifully, a sense of humour did eventually return when it was claimed that the excellent drink was 'Made in Scotland from girders.' Of course it is.

27

The Papers

In January 1783 a printer called John Mennons found he had a global scoop on his hands, and he had to hold, as it turned out, not the front page but the back page. As he was compositing the very first edition of a weekly publication with the masthead of 'The Glasgow Advertiser', Mennons happened to speak to the lord provost – who told him that the Peace of Paris had been agreed between Great Britain and the thirteen colonies who had fought for and won their independence. The treaty brought into being the United States of America. This momentous story appeared not on the front page, because Mennons had already laid it out, but instead on the back page, in a larger font, in the space he had left for late news. In 1802 the enterprising printer sold the *Glasgow Advertiser* and it became the *Herald and Advertiser and Commercial Chronicle* before that mouthful mercifully changed into the *Glasgow Herald* three years later. It is now the longest-running newspaper in the world and, give or take a month or two, as old as the United States of America.

In 1968 it was reckoned that more Scots read more newspapers than any other country in the world. Published in Dundee but with several local editions, mainly for sports reports, the *Sunday Post* is perhaps the most striking illustration of Scotland's historic love affair with the papers. In that year, its readership reached a peak of just over 3 million,

80 per cent of all Scots. Cartoon strips 'Oor Wullie' and 'The Broons' were read by younger Scots as they plucked the Fun Section out of the main paper. And, in 1983, a survey found that 84.6 per cent of all adults in Scotland read a morning paper, compared to 75 per cent in England. So there. There are in fact historical reasons for this. In large part because of the Reformation doctrine of the priesthood of all believers and its insistence on a school in every parish, mass literacy was higher and came earlier than in any other country in the late nineteenth and early twentieth centuries.

While Dundee's *Sunday Post* used to dominate and its publisher, D. C. Thomson, still produces it and the *Dundee Evening Telegraph* in the city, Glasgow is where most of Scotland's newspapers originate. The *Herald*'s sister paper is the *Glasgow Evening Times*, and there are Scottish editions of *The Times*, the *Sun*, the *Daily Mail* and the *Mail on Sunday*. The tabloid that used to dominate the weekday market was the *Daily Record*, and as late as 2005, it sold 454,427 copies each day, a readership of perhaps 1.5 million. In a very short time all of these circulation figures crashed, and now only 52,264 copies of the *Daily Record* are sold each day. The *Herald* (having dropped 'Glasgow' in 1992) has a daily circulation of only 11,364 now compared with 58,000 in 2005 and double that number in the 1980s.

Arguably, the decline in newspaper sales began with radio and then TV sports reporting. Comprehensive weekend football results in particular were only available in what were known as the Saturday pink papers published in Glasgow, Edinburgh and Dundee. But when football pools fillers, clutching their coupons, could discover whether or not they were winners or losers by watching sports round-ups on TV at around 5 p.m. on a Saturday, there was no longer any need to queue up outside the newsagent to wait for the bundles of pinks to arrive from the railway station.

When. on 4 November 1997, the BBC launched BBC News Online, that service quickly eroded newspaper circulation. It was free, immediate and continually updated. By 2005 the online service was reaching 12 million users a month, but by April 2021 BBC News Online had 1.2 billion website visits in a single month. Newspapers launched their own sites, and to some extent that staunched the bleeding. But advertising, the major source of income for the papers, also began to migrate online, where it was often much cheaper and reached more people. Social media platforms like Facebook carrying news compounded the problems, and newspapers were forced to shed staff and compromise the quality and quantity of what they published. And when smartphone cameras improved sufficiently to be able to shoot decent, if sometimes shaky, footage, that brought major incidents to the internet no reporter could hope to report. And that, in turn, brought more people seeking the first-hand drama of accidents, natural disasters and even assaults and murders to the internet.

While all of these developments represent real and continuing threats to the survival of the papers, the major casualties have been standards: honesty, a lack of bias and balanced reporting. Industry regulation and the laws of defamation in particular did not always work, but their presence did go some way to preserving standards of journalism. On the internet, anything goes. And that can be tremendously damaging to the fabric of societies that seemed robust even ten years ago. In 2024 a presidential election was fought in the USA where the Republican candidate lied repeatedly, invented stories almost daily and insulted his opponent as well as many others. He suffered only ridicule and, in the campaign, little or no backlash. Many people have become habituated to lies, what one presidential aide called 'alternative facts'. Voters who get all their news from the internet, which also has no filter, have become conditioned to believe almost anything. Absurd conspiracy theories abound, and online search engines are now portals to a maze of lies and deceptions. The diminishment and even loss of the papers is not a matter of nostalgia for a simpler past: it is much to be regretted.

28

Doon the Watter

Millions of Glaswegians have good reason to be grateful to Bishop Jocelin, even if they have no idea who he was. When, in 1190, he persuaded King William the Lion to allow Glasgow to have a fair, it began life in the cathedral precinct but eventually lit up the lives of generations of Glaswegians. Held in the middle of July, the Fair became an annual holiday, enjoyed from Fair Friday and over the weekend following. The traditional livestock sales were soon augmented and eventually taken over by what we might think of as fairground attractions, known as 'the shows' in Scotland. In 1917 these even included a simulation of what life in the Ypres trenches was like, with a full-sized reproduction of the dugouts, hospitals and dressing stations – a somewhat sobering nod to a grim reality amidst all the penny arcades and the candy floss. The Fair was held on Glasgow Green (and other large public spaces) and many thousands came to compete for teddy bears and goldfish in a bag.

Before and after the First World War, MacBrayne ferries and other maritime traffic were busy as Glaswegians increasingly went 'doon the watter', down the Firth of Clyde to Rothesay, Troon, Largs, Millport, Brodick, Ayr and the other seaside towns that were quickly developing into resorts. By the end of the previous century, working people could afford trips aboard the passenger steamers, on the weekend after Fair

Friday, and since almost all businesses and factories closed for the holiday, the boats were very crowded indeed. Neil Munro was the editor of the *Glasgow Evening News* and also the author of the famous and enduring Para Handy tales of the skipper of a puffer, *The Vital Spark*, that plied up and down the Firth of Clyde and around the Hebrides. Here is an atmospheric description from one of the early stories about a day trip up Loch Fyne that was published in the *Glasgow Evening News*:

> The last passenger steamer to sail that day from Ardrishaig was a trip from Rothesay. It was Glasgow Fair Saturday and Ardrishaig Quay was black with people. There was a marvelously stimulating odour of dulse, herring and shell-fish, for everybody carried away in a handkerchief a few samples of these marine products that are now the only sea-side souvenirs not made in Germany. The *Vital Spark* in ballast, Clydeward bound, lay inside the passenger steamer, ready to start when the latter had got under weight, and Para Handy and his mate meanwhile sat on the fo'c'sle-head of 'the smertest boat in the tred [trade]' watching the frantic efforts of lady excursionists to get their husbands on the steamer before it was too late, and the deliberate efforts of the said husbands to slink away up the village again just for one more drink. Wildly the steamer hooted from her siren, fiercely clanged her bell, vociferously the captain roared on his bridge, people on board yelled eagerly to friends ashore to hurry up, and the people ashore as eagerly demanded to know what all the hurry was about, and where the bleezes was Wull? Women loudly defied the purser to let the ship go away without their John, for he had paid his money for his ticket, and though he was only a working-man his money was as good as anybody else's; and John, on the

> quay, with his hat thrust back on his head, his thumbs in the arm-hole of his waistcoat and a red handkerchief full of dulse at his feet, gave display of step-dancing that was responsible for a great deal of the congestion of traffic at the shore end of the gangway.

In 1938, after a twenty-year campaign of political pressure from the trade union movement, the government agreed to the Holidays with Pay Act. This entitled workers to one week of paid leave. It was later extended to a fortnight. The Second World War intervened, and it was not until the later 1940s that working people and their families could enjoy Fair Fortnight to the full. Most went doon the watter on day trips, and, increasingly, more and more were able to afford to stay in guesthouses and other accommodation. Billy Butlin's holiday camp at Ayr was very popular. The heyday of the Clyde resorts was in the 1950s and early 1960s before the lure of cheap package holidays to Spain and the guaranteed sunshine of the Mediterranean. Some of these old seaside resorts have become somewhat forlorn as the echoes of families on Fair Friday swirl around their windy promenades.

29

Red Clydeside

Three photographs have prompted many thousands of words, many of them misleading. On Friday 31 January 1919, a huge crowd gathered in George Square to demonstrate their support for a strike called to persuade employers to introduce a forty-hour working week. One photograph shows a packed sea of bunnets, the faces under them all turned towards a red flag flying above the throng. At the bottom of the picture there is a ring of helmeted policemen, and one of them has turned to look at the photographer, and not kindly. Two other photographs were taken in quick succession outside the City Chambers. The first shows a man lying on his back on the pavement, being tended to by one policemen and a friend. He was Davie Kirkwood, one of the organisers of the strike, and another photo shows him being arrested. His head is bowed, and a policeman holds him by the collar and at his wrist. Another man, who might be Willie Gallacher, has a bandage on his head; both are dwarfed by the big Glasgow polis. These images have fed a version of events that spoke of working people fighting for their rights against a brutal police force backed by detachments of soldiers, machine guns and tanks sent by the government in London to protect and patrol the streets of Glasgow. That day in January was the moment when revolution might have flared, when the Clyde might have turned red.

The historical truth is somewhat different. There is no doubt that the government were nervous, for they had good reason. There had been revolution in Dublin with the Easter Rising of 1916, revolution and the overthrow of the Tsar in Russia in 1917, and after the end of the First World War, there was violence on the streets of Berlin, Munich and the Baltic ports as bloody clashes between left- and right-wing factions broke out. The great fear was that Bolshevism was contagious.

There had been unease on Clydeside throughout the war. Not only were there rent strikes, with the abuse of sheriff officers and rent collectors; there had also been a series of strikes in the shipyards. Wages were very low, the working hours very long, and the Clyde Workers' Committee was formed to fight for their rights. But the country was engaged in a brutal, grinding war, and the government saw the CWC's activities as contrary to the Defence of the Realm Act. Their leaders were arrested, charged with sedition and 'court-martialled'. In 1916 Willie Gallacher, James Maxton, John Maclean and others were incarcerated in Calton Jail in Edinburgh while Davie Kirkwood was confined to the city. He later breached that order by travelling to a conference in Manchester and was locked up in Edinburgh Castle.

After the First World War, the demand for shipping and munitions collapsed and unemployment soared. So that more men could be employed, the CWC argued that the working week should be shortened. The engineering trade unions and the employers agreed on a forty-seven-hour week, but the CWC insisted on forty. There was no agreement, and the unions declared a strike, beginning on 27 January 1919. More than 70,000 workers came out and mass pickets tried to persuade others to join them. The tram workers refused, and in the background to the famous red flag photograph, the silhouette of a tram can be made out. The focus of the campaign was to be a mass rally in George Square on 31 January 1919. Fearing serious trouble, Lord Provost James Stewart sent a telegram to the War Cabinet in Westminster seeking advice, and help if possible.

Stewart's plea had a mixed reception. The War Cabinet was inclined to see the Clydeside strike as a local matter. But the Secretary of State for Scotland, Robert Munro, was more fearful, as was the Sheriff of Lanarkshire, Alastair Mackenzie, and it was he who raised the proposal to send troops to Glasgow to back up the police, armed only with truncheons. General Sir William Robertson, the only soldier ever to rise from the rank of private to field marshal, pointed out that the army's 'aid to the civil power' depended on local sheriffs explicitly asking for it. And they had not. The initiative lay with local authorities. At that time the Secretary of State for War, Winston Churchill, far from being the instigator of army involvement, as is often asserted, thought that Munro and Mackenzie were making too much of the threat. He suggested that, like Maxton, Wheatley, Kirkwood and Gallacher in 1916, the leaders of the strike should again be arrested under the Defence of the Realm Act. Eventually, the War Cabinet agreed to form a three-man committee to handle the situation: Robert Munro, the Lord Advocate, James Clyde and Robert Horne, the MP for Glasgow Hillhead. Major-General Sir Wyndham Childs, who had dealt with conscientious objectors during the war, acted as a military advisor. These were the men who influenced events, and not Winston Churchill.

The day dawned, and crowds of strikers gathered in George Square. Many accounts exaggerate the numbers wildly, saying that between 70,000 and 100,000 crammed into the square, a physical impossibility. In the red flag photograph, there is clearly open space beyond the crowd of bunnets, with what might be young boys looking on. The police estimated 25,000 to 30,000. Before the fiery speeches began, the CWC leadership (Davie Kirkwood, Willie Gallacher and Manny Shinwell, later a long-serving Labour MP and cabinet minister) went into the City Chambers to seek a meeting with John Stewart. Stupidly, the lord provost kept them waiting because he was in a meeting with councillors. While the three men waited, the crowd outside grew restless, the mood intensified, and the police became more and more anxious. There were only 140 on duty, and they could have been overwhelmed. Damage had already been done by the crowd in the streets around George Square: shop windows smashed, some looting and a lorry loaded with bottles overturned, its cargo used as missiles to throw at the police.

It must have seemed as though things were teetering on a knife's edge. Sheriff Alastair Mackenzie had formally requested military intervention, but no troops would arrive in Glasgow until 10 p.m. that night. And contrary to some of the mythology that swirls around the events of the day, they were not exclusively English. Most were Scots, detachments from the Seaforth Highlanders, the King's Own Scottish Borderers, the Argyll and Southern Highlanders and the Royal Scots. It was also claimed that the Highland Light Infantry had been locked in their barracks to prevent them joining the fray – on the wrong side. But in fact they were not in Glasgow at that time. And nor were there tanks on the streets of Glasgow on 31 January. Six were in the city, but tucked away in the Cattle Market, off the Gallowgate. Stories of machine guns positioned on buildings and artillery on street corners were overwrought fantasy.

By noon, with the leaders still inside the City Chambers, the crowd in George Square was becoming increasingly agitated. There were clashes with the police, and Sheriff Alastair Mackenzie began to read the riot act. But before he could finish, a striker snatched it out of his hands. Seeing what was kicking off, Gallacher, Kirkwood and Shinwell rushed out of the City Chambers to try to calm things down. But by that time events had got out of hand. The crowd and the police were scuffling, and many, including officers, took some nasty knocks. Davie Kirkwood was felled by a truncheon and knocked unconscious while Manny Shinwell fled into the nearby CWC office. By about 3.30 p.m., when it was getting dark, the disturbances had begun to die down and the crowd eventually dispersed. Twelve were arrested and tried for a variety of offences. Most were acquitted; only Shinwell and Gallacher and two others were found guilty and sentenced to a few months in jail.

Instead of revolution, the CWC leadership chose a democratic route to power. Kirkwood, Shinwell, Wheatley and Maxton became MPs. Willie Gallacher went to Russia, met Lenin and came back to Britain to build the new Communist Party of Great Britain. In 1935 he became the Communist MP for West Fife and held the seat until 1950. It should also be remembered that Glasgow's politics reached across the political spectrum. In 1922 Labour won ten of the city's seats, but the others were held by four Conservatives and a Liberal. The incoming prime minister, Andrew Bonar Law, schooled and raised in Glasgow, won the seat of Glasgow Central.

30

The Clydebank Blitz

Isa Mackenzie never forgot the night of 13 March 1941. Twelve years old, she lived with her parents and twin brother Donald in a top-floor flat near the railway station at Clydebank. She was getting ready to go to bed at about 9 p.m. when the air raid sirens sounded over the town:

> My father got us dressed in our best coats and took us downstairs into the hallway of a room-and-kitchen flat on the ground floor. One lady stayed at the front entrance, and whenever she heard a bomb whistle, she would shout, 'Duck!' and we would all have to get down. When we heard the slap, slap, slap, slap we thought it was tiles falling from the roof, but it was the incendiary bombs.
>
> We were there for five hours, and then the lady shouted, 'You'll have to get out. The building's on fire.' We tried the brick shelters, but they were only half built, with walls but no roofs.
>
> As we were running, aircraft were strafing us with bullets. People didn't believe us, but next day there were bullet marks on the buildings. Eventually, we made it to a billiards room. There were lots of people there already, including an elderly lady, plus mattress, on top of the billiard table. The owners of the cornershop brought in biscuits and sweets.

> At 7 a.m. the all-clear went. We came out to discover our building was rubble. The kitchen range was hanging off the wall. That was all that was left of our house . . . We didn't know where to go. Mum and Dad had been married for twenty-seven years, and that was everything they owned. There were no trams, no trains, big holes in the road. We got a lorry to take us to our aunt's in Scotstoun. She fed us and let us sleep in their beds. We had been up for twenty-four hours . . .
>
> I broke down on the bus. It was like being in a horror film, passing the Singer wood yard and the [oil storage] tanks and Bowling, and the whole place was just flames. This was something we had never thought about. We had seen it in the news in the cinemas, Coventry and London, but we never gave it a thought that one day it would be us.

On the nights of 13 and 14 March 1941 waves of Luftwaffe bombers attacked Clydebank and its shipyards and munitions factories. Four hundred and thirty-nine aircraft dropped more than 272 tonnes of bombs and 1,650 of the incendiary bombs that Isa Mackenzie could hear so clearly. For nine hours the Heinkel bombers pounded the town. The impact was utter devastation. Official estimates are only that, and instead of almost 600, it is now believed that more than 1,200 people were killed, approximately 1,000 seriously injured and hundreds more hit by blast debris. The town was all but erased. Out of roughly 12,000 houses, only eight remained intact. Four thousand were reduced to rubble, a further 4,500 badly damaged and 3,500 suffered more minor damage. The raid was described as 'the most cataclysmic event' in Scotland during the Second World War.

The Luftwaffe had flown on moonless nights, their navigators guided by the glint off the River Clyde, and their main targets on 13 March were the Singer sewing machine factory (it had been adapted to manufacture weapons), John Brown's shipyard and the Royal Ordnance Factory at Dalmuir. These and the oil storage tanks Isa saw blazing were all badly damaged. But the reason that the town suffered so severely was that so much housing was located very near the yards and factories. On 14 March the Luftwaffe mounted a second raid, and it was a terror raid, aimed at civilians, intended to sap morale. It failed. And all the death and destruction of those terrible nights turned out to have a benign legacy. Not only did it motivate the men and women on the home front to work harder for victory in the war, but it also helped to win the peace.

Mindful of the unrest and the strikes in Glasgow during the First World War, Winston Churchill wisely gave control of those ministries that ran the home front to Labour politicians. Before he accepted the role of Secretary of State for Scotland, Tom Johnston demanded what amounted to vice-regal powers, and he used them. After the shock and devastation of the Clydebank Blitz, Johnston set up the Emergency Hospital Service. If there were going to be more raids, then existing hospitals would be overwhelmed. And he also realised that any new provision should be well away from centres of population that might become targets. New hospitals were quickly built at Raigmore near Inverness, Stracathro near Brechin, Bridge of Earn in Perthshire, Killearn in Stirlingshire, Law in North Lanarkshire, Ballochmyle in Ayrshire and at Peel in the Borders. Several stayed in use until the 1980s. New annexes were also built onto existing hospitals, and some of Scotland's most luxurious hotels were commandeered as convalescent facilities. As one of the radical MPs who left St Enoch Station in 1922, that may have made Tom Johnston smile.

When it became clear that there would probably be no more raids on the scale that had hit Clydebank, Johnston decided that civilians waiting for scarce medical care should be treated in the new hospitals free of charge. Waiting lists disappeared, and by the end of the war about 33,000 civilian patients had been looked after. Johnston also launched the Clyde Basin Scheme, an innovative experiment in preventative medicine, and it was later extended across Scotland. In total, the Emergency Hospital Scheme provided an additional 20,500 hospital beds and 30 per cent more nurses than in England as well as more GPs. Tom Johnston had laid the foundations of the National Health Service and showed how it would work.

31

The Dock and the Firth

Using its geographical location as an Atlantic port, its generations of shipping and engineering experience and all its innovative, improvising skills, the Second City of the Empire exacted sustained retribution for the death and destruction that rained down on Clydebank. From October 1942, the course of the Second World War turned as the allies turned from defence to begin a series of offensive operations. Glasgow had a central, pivotal role in preparing seaborne attacks on Nazi-occupied Europe and North Africa, and also as a port of arrival for the thousands of American and Canadian soldiers who crossed the Atlantic to join the war against fascism.

The first of these was Operation Torch. Planned as a series of Anglo-American landings in North Africa, at Casablanca, Oran and Algiers, the lynchpin of the expeditions was the largest dock on the Upper Clyde and the deepwater anchorage at the Tail o' the Bank, off Greenock. The King George V dock, known as KG5, was both the muster point and embarkation point for soldiers, armament and supplies. It lay on the edge of Govan, with green fields beyond it. Very large, it could accommodate ten troopships at any given time, and it was also served by a railway that brought men and materials very close to the quayside and the long embarkation sheds that had been built close to the dock. This compact arrangement was important in two ways. It made the transfer of troops easy and quick, and it hid operations from view, both from the sky and the land. Security was vital if the landings in North Africa were to achieve a degree of surprise, and soldiers were left in no doubt about its importance by posters plastered on the walls of the sheds:

> ON ARRIVAL
> Do not talk about the ship or whence she sailed or when.
> Do not say what ships were seen on the voyage.
> Only tell your friends of incidents within the ship in your letters and do not mention the name of the ship.
> Never give away the names or the descriptions of other ships in company or of friendly aircraft that may have been seen.
> Tittle tattle, idle gossip, and giving credence to rumours may endanger the vessel in which you have now so many friends.

Built at Fairfield's yard in 1937, the passenger-cargo liner, the *Circassia*, had been converted into an armed merchant cruiser. It joined the task force for Operation Torch at KG5 before sailing downriver to the Tail o' the Bank anchorage where it met the larger transports of the Clyde Task Force. With more than 300 ships, it was the largest fleet ever seen on the river. At the mouth of the Firth of Clyde, there was a rendezvous with the Eastern Task Force from Northern Ireland before the long voyage to North Africa. The captain of the *Circassia* was David Bone, who described the scene in his 1949 memoir, *Merchantman Re-armed*:

> Military Embarkation Dock [KG5], at which troops were marched on board ship up a long, sloping gangway (or brow) whose other end might ultimately rest on Norway,

Africa, India, Burma or Australia, wherever the fortune of the day required them. It is sufficiently remote from the city and public observation of troop movements. A network of railway lines flows into it on the western side and it was generally in darkness the long troop trains drew into or hauled out from the dockside on rail connection with all parts of the Kingdom.

On 10 July 1943, Operation Husky saw Allied landings on Sicily, and again Glasgow was centrally involved. The *Circassia* carried fourteen flat-bottomed landing craft slung from specially made davits on the upper deck, double-banked to get as many on board as possible. Their crew of three and the thirty-five soldiers each could carry had spent the early part of that summer training on the beaches of Lamlash and Brodick in Arran, Inveraray and Loch Fyne. Many were Americans and Canadians who had crossed the Atlantic in liners like the *Queen Mary* and *Queen Elizabeth*, both returning to the Clyde yards, where they were built after having been refitted as troopships. In early 1944 HMS *Puncher*, an aircraft carrier acquired from the USA under the lend-lease scheme, arrived at KG5 heavily loaded with fighter aircraft lashed to the flight deck. Other ships brought fighters or fighter-bombers in crates. These were unloaded at the dock and transported by rail to Abbotsinch, only a short distance away, where they were assembled, fuelled and flown to wherever they were needed.

In 1944 Glasgow saw two remarkable structures that would play a vital role in Operation Overlord, the code name for the Normandy landings planned for June of that year. These were the ingenious Mulberry harbours. Assembled in Lanarkshire at the Parkneuk steel works in Motherwell and towed by ships down the Firth of Clyde, these were crucial to the supply of the troops who had stormed the beaches, and who could not wait for an existing, heavily defended Channel port to be captured. Winston Churchill described them:

> A large area of sheltered water protected by a breakwater based on blockships brought to the scene by their own power and then sunk in a prearranged position . . .
>
> The whole project was majestic. On the beaches themselves would be the great piers, with their seaward ends afloat and sheltered. At these piers coasters and landing craft would be able to discharge at all states of the tide.

In charge of this vital part of the invasion was Rear-Admiral Harold Hickling, and he was in no doubt about the importance of these floating harbours: 'The whole success of the invasion depended on the "Mulberry", and without it they could have no guarantee that the vital supplies for our armed forces could have been landed.'

There can be no debate that Glasgow's skills and engineering know-how played a vital role in turning the tide of the Second World War. It was now time to win the peace and make the city a place fit for heroes who had served abroad and those who had worked so hard along the banks of the Clyde.

32

Gorbals No More

Taken sometime in the late 1960s, there exists a photograph that captures a period of radical change. A beautiful Gothic church, with a hall and what seem to be houses for its priests, stands on a street corner. Or rather on a corner where there used to be streets. On three sides, St Francis Church is surrounded by open ground. There is no grass, no trees or hedges, just what seem to be temporary wooden fences and two rows of streetlights. Overshadowing the church on one side are two massive tower blocks of flats, ten storeys high, each with a balcony. Only just visible are two people standing on the highest balcony. They were looking out over the Gorbals, a once densely packed residential area of Glasgow's city centre.

Another photograph, this one taken in 1955, remembers what the view used to be like. The cameraman looks down over the cobbles of Mathieson Street, a major thoroughfare through the district. Other photos, probably taken on the same overcast day, show a continuous line of four-storey tenements, many of the frontages in poor condition, streaked with the leaks from broken rainwater downpipes, their closemouths scarred by graffiti and many of the windows with only scraps of net rather than curtains. The street cobbles have frayed badly at the edges and left puddles where drainage has been obstructed. Across the street from St Francis is a curious, slightly ramshackle building. Converted from a church hall, it is the Paragon Picture House. It seated a staggering 1,319, and the photograph was taken just before it was closed in 1958 after the elderly doorman was stabbed to death.

Some of these photographs, and others like them, appear on Facebook groups, and often the members exchange messages that are sticky with nostalgia for the communities of the old neighbourhoods. They recount tales of how people helped each other out and in general pine for the old days, when life was simpler. For Frances Walker, life in the Gorbals was a version of hell. She lived in a single-end, what was in essence a one-room flat that was rarely larger than fourteen feet square, and often smaller. Born in the Gorbals in 1938, Frances emigrated with her family to Australia in 1963. Her rage at her early upbringing burned for the rest of her life. Here is an extract from an interview she gave in 1999:

> Can I say now that it was hell living in Mathieson Street? My father was in the RAF serving in India but he rarely sent us any money. We were seven in one room. We had one cold water tap when the pipes were not burst and shared one toilet with all of the close. At night when all the beds were down the only things that could move were the rats and, believe me, they ran all over us. The rat-catcher came one night, and in our single-end, he caught fourteen. I almost lost my leg in a rat bite. It took months to heal. We never had enough to eat – to be honest, we were starving. I have a few photographs of us slum kids in the back courts – we looked like tinkers.

The stench of poverty was everywhere in the Gorbals. With a population density of 281 per acre, about the size of a football pitch, it was almost impossible to escape it. Forty thousand lived in a tiny inner city area. Decaying, rotting tenements like those in Mathieson Street and their overflowing communal toilets was another unwelcome constant. Overcrowding was at its worst in Glasgow and the industrial towns of the lower Clyde Valley. The Census of 1951 revealed that of all those in Scotland who lived in single-ends, 49 per cent were in Glasgow, while in Edinburgh, Dundee and Aberdeen only 16 per cent of their total population were crammed into one room. And when Glasgow's baleful statistics were isolated, it showed that 50.5 per cent of all Glaswegians lived in flats with only one or two rooms. Frances Walker's experience was not unique.

With Labour's landslide election victory in 1945, action to deal with this vast housing crisis was taken immediately. There was no other choice. With the return of demobbed soldiers, sailors and airmen, and the passing of the Family Allowances Act, the post-war baby boom began. In and around Glasgow there were two competing solutions to the problem. The Clyde Valley Regional Plan of 1946, drafted by Sir Patrick Abercrombie and Robert H. Matthew, was radical in its approach. Populations would be decanted to live in new towns built beyond Glasgow's boundaries, with good transport links to take them back and forth to the city to work. East Kilbride was the first, in 1947; Cumbernauld followed in 1956. Other families, who were, somewhat uncharitably, labelled 'Glasgow Overspill' would be relocated to towns across Scotland to houses built by the Scottish Special Housing Association.

Unhappy about the city losing a large proportion of its population, and consequently a lot of its political clout, Robert Bruce, the Master of Works and the City Engineer, came up with an alternative. All of the 316,000 new homes that were needed could be built within Glasgow's boundaries.

But only if the majority were not houses but flats, both low- and high-rise. Glasgow Corporation began the construction of four huge schemes on the periphery of the city at Pollok, Castlemilk, Drumchapel and Easterhouse. By 1951 most of the building work (but not the infrastructure) at Pollok was complete. The majority of the new residents came from the Gorbals or Govan. One woman later recalled:

> We were on the waiting list for over fourteen years. When you were offered a house, you jumped at it.
>
> It was pretty grim and cold when we first arrived in 1947. The gardens were all bare, no streetlights and the roads were dirt tracks. But it was great to get away from the smoke of the Gorbals though it took us a while to get used to it out here.

Most important to all who moved were not so much the surroundings but the flat itself:

> We moved from a room and kitchen to this four-apartment. It was great to have hot running water and an inside toilet for the first time.
>
> The one thing that stood out was the bathroom. It made a change from having to get washed in an old bathtub.

High tower blocks were built elsewhere in the city, but many of these were unsuccessful, poorly built at speed and simply too high. Glasgow's climate came off the Atlantic and at fifteen or twenty storeys, the wind howled around these flats. Tenants complained that the noise made it impossible to hear the radio or the TV or even talk to each other. Building standards could be poor, with damp and a lack of insulation causing chronic difficulties. Some tower blocks began to fall apart with half-ton sheets of cladding coming away from the fabric because of rusting fixtures. But there were also successes. Families coming from the inner-city slums were delighted with their new accommodation, especially the hot and cold running water, private toilets and bathrooms, and heating that was efficient.

Many of the tower blocks had short lives and were demolished only decades after they were built. And some of the housing schemes like Easterhouse became notorious. But it should be borne in mind that Glasgow had an enormous problem in 1945 and the city's officials and councillors acted as they did from the best of motives. In order to get families out of the rat-infested, foul-smelling slums of the Gorbals and elsewhere, they moved quickly and decisively, if not always effectively. But they were determined that no child should have the upbringing that Frances Walker was forced to endure.

33

Palaces of Dreams

Mary McCusker was born in the Gorbals in 1916 in the shadow of St Francis, and her memories of escaping the realities of life in the crumbling tenements were vivid:

> The Paragon was the local cinema in Cumberland Street . . . a wee fleapit sort of style . . . penny matinee on a Saturday. I can remember this particular film, *Dr Fu Manchu*. And that night I came home and had a nightmare about Dr Fu Manchu. The Chinese man with the big, long nails. And my mother vowed that was the last picture I was ever to see. I was never to get back again. Both of them were up all night with me with this nightmare. I could see him walking through the kitchen. Just shows you.
>
> Then we had another cinema, the Crown Picture House in Crown Street. We went there on a Saturday morning, the matinee. And if you went upstairs you got an American coloured comic . . . Upstairs was tuppence . . . it was a penny downstairs.

Mary never lost the habit of going to the pictures.

> I remember *Viennese Nights*. Oh! It was lovely. And I think Alexander Gray and Vivienne Segal were the stars of it . . . Oh we were on the beautiful seats and everything . . . Further

> down Maryhill Road there was the Blythswood, the Seamore, the Cambridge, along Cambridge Street. And these were the picture halls we went to, my husband and I . . . Some of them were epics . . . and Barbara Stanwyck in a picture called *So Big*. Marvellous, marvellous, stories. Could be remakes, you know, if they only had the sense to remake them.

In fact, the Paragon, a cinema with a capacity of more than a thousand can scarcely be described as 'a fleapit'. The scale of Glasgow's picture houses was grand. In the 1930s, there were more than 130, and the city had the highest ratio of cinema seats per head of population in Europe. Glasgow's love affair with the pictures began in May 1896 in a surprising way. The first footage to be shown was of course silent, but also very much in the background, more of a marketing gimmick. Arthur Hubner's Real Ice Skating Palace opened in Sauchiehall Street, and it featured seven short films played on a loop and accompanied by an orchestra as skaters skated across the ice. In 1907 Pringle's Picture House opened in a converted Queen's Theatre. Perhaps one of the longest runs was La Scala, also in Sauchiehall Street. It opened in 1912 and closed in 1984 after many refurbishments.

Cinemas used to run their features in a continuous loop, and early audiences were in the habit of buying a ticket at any time and watching films that might be halfway through. It seemed not to spoil anyone's enjoyment to watch one film end and then wait for it to start again so that they could see how it began. Once ticket buyers had seen the whole film, the timeless phrase that now applies to many things came into use: 'This is where we came in.'

The longest-running survivor of the great era of cinema in cinema city is the Glasgow Film Theatre. It opened as a smaller, 'arthouse' theatre in 1939 and is still running. But, sadly, Glasgow's greatest filmmaker was persuaded to have the premiere of his first film, *That Sinking Feeling*, at the Edinburgh Film Festival in 1979. Set in the Calton, Bridgeton and Parkhead areas, Bill Forsyth's comedy about a group of unemployed teenagers who steal seventy-four stainless steel sinks and try to sell them was an unlikely and immediate success. Made for only £5,000, it starred members of the Glasgow Youth Theatre and did well enough to lead to *Gregory's Girl*. The main location of this school-based comedy was Cumbernauld, and it starred John Gordon Sinclair, Dee Hepburn and Clare Grogan, with Chic Murray as the long-suffering, piano-playing headmaster. It in turn made possible Forsyth's greatest commercial hit, *Local Hero*, and after that, *Comfort and Joy*. Starring Bill Paterson as a local disc jockey caught up in the struggle between two Italian families over the sale of ice cream in Glasgow, it is brilliant. Perhaps Forsyth's best film, it captures perfectly the atmosphere of the city in the 1980s. In an excellent cameo, Rikki Fulton played Hilary, the managing director of Glasgow's commercial radio station. His long and versatile career spanned all of the entertainment media – film, TV and radio – but it took off in what was a Glasgow institution in the 1950s and 1960s.

The *Five-Past Eight* show began at the Alhambra Theatre in Wellington Street and was billed as a 'fast-moving singing, dancing and laughter show' starring Jimmy Logan and Jack Radcliffe with Kenneth McKellar, the singer of 'The Song Of The Clyde'. By 1956 Stanley Baxter and Rikki Fulton were filling the 2,800-seat theatre. With Jack Milroy, Fulton created two memorable Glaswegian characters. Francie and Josie were a cross between Teddy Boys and Mods who wore loud suits (with the trouser legs a touch too short) and eccentric haircuts. Between them, often improvising, Milroy and Fulton created a mythic, comic version of the city.

While the Alhambra rocked with the laughter of recognition at the patter and antics of Francie and Josie, audiences could be merciless with performers they did not like. The Empire Theatre on Sauchiehall Street was notorious as 'the graveyard of English comedians', especially the second house on a Friday or Saturday night after the pubs had closed. Des O'Connor was so intimidated by the jeering that he pretended to faint and had to be dragged off the stage by the ankles. When in the 1960s one half of a famous double act, Mike Winters, wandered on, playing his clarinet, he was greeted with a stunned silence. But when his brother, Bernie, appeared, a lone voice rang through the theatre: 'Oh Christ, there's two of them.'

Between 1862 and the outbreak of war in 1914, eighteen theatres were built in Glasgow, such was the popular demand for live entertainment. Her Majesty's Theatre was the first to be located on the south side of the city, in the heart of the Gorbals. In 1943 the successful playwright James Bridie helped form the Citizens Theatre Company with a clear manifesto 'to make Glasgow independent from London for its dramatic supplies . . . [and to] produce plays which the Glasgow playgoers would otherwise not have the opportunity of seeing'. Two years later Bridie's company moved to the Royal Princess Theatre (formerly Her Majesty's) in the Gorbals. In its first twenty-one years, the Citz, as it quickly and affectionately became known, produced almost 300 plays. Seventy-two of them were British or World premieres. James Bridie was also a central figure in the Royal Scottish Academy of Music's establishment of a drama department, and it eventually became the Royal Conservatoire of Scotland.

34

What's on Channel 10, Hen?

In 1953 the live broadcast of the coronation of Queen Elizabeth II (of England, but I of Scotland) boosted the sale of TV sets, and for the first time, very large audiences watched. More than 2.1 million households had a TV licence in Britain at that time. What changed and expanded viewing dramatically was the rental market. Sets, often called receivers in those early days, were very expensive to buy, but companies like Radio Rentals and DER began to offer much more affordable deals, both hire purchase and rentals, and by 1960 the number of households with a TV licence had increased to 9.3 million.

In 1954 the Conservative Government approved proposals to bring commercial television into being after pressure had persuaded them that TV advertising would stimulate retail demand and therefore the economy. On 31 August 1957 Scottish Television began broadcasting. Based at the Theatre Royal in Glasgow, the station was originally known as Channel 10 because that's where it sat on the dial of the TV sets of the period.

The centrepiece of the opening evening was a live programme called *This Is Scotland*. It was a strange mash-up of items introduced by the actor James Robertson Justice. Within a few awkward, halting moments, it became clear that he had either forgotten his lines or could not read the cue cards under the camera lens, and so he was forced to read from a script. There was then a largely meaningless meander around some film of the bens and the glens with a stirring voice-over that spoke of 'misty glens' and 'lusty streams', whatever they were. That then gave way to a performance on the stage of the Theatre Royal. The singer Kenneth McKellar stood on a high podium while various figures in costume jigged and reeled around him. One was dressed as a shepherd, and another appeared to be a gamekeeper carrying a shotgun. Perhaps someone prayed that he would use it. And what the inhabitants of Govan, Partick and Castlemilk made of all this cavorting around, a gaggle of Highland countryside clichés that had nothing whatever to do with their lives in the city, can only be guessed at.

Despite this uncertain start, Channel 10 became what Lady Plowden, the chair of the ITV regulator, called 'distressingly popular'. *The One O'Clock Gang*, presented by Larry Marshall, was a sketch and song show broadcast live from the Theatre Royal in Glasgow. Unlike the BBC, most of whose output came from London, it was definitely, unmistakably, Scottish, done unapologetically in Glasgow accents. Larry Marshall and the other presenters went down into the audience and talked to them. Suddenly ordinary people could be on TV. From the stage the cast read out viewers' letters, usually marking anniversaries and birthdays. Thousands of editions were broadcast. *The One O'Clock Gang* was a programme about us, not one that featured posh people, not like the BBC. There was not a cut-glass accent within earshot.

The founding consortium who were awarded the franchise to broadcast in central Scotland (the north would later be served by Grampian TV and the south by Border TV) was headed by a Canadian businessman, Roy Thomson. Initially, he held 80 per cent of the share capital and was thereby in complete control of the company. The agreement with the ITV regulator was that what soon became STV would be allowed initially to broadcast fifty hours of programmes a week, ten of which would be produced in Glasgow and central Scotland. Conveniently, *The One O'Clock Gang* accounted for many of those home-produced hours. One of the first series to be broadcast was *Fanfare*, a sporting quiz show in which teams from the supporters' clubs of Scotland's professional football teams competed. Advertising sales were buoyant, and Roy Thomson made the ill-advised remark that having an ITV franchise was like 'a licence to print money'. Sadly, he used most of the profits elsewhere in his media empire to invest in the *Scotsman* newspaper and others he owned.

In 1965 the chairman of the Independent Television Authority, Charles Hill, visited the STV studios at the Theatre Royal and watched an edition of *The One O'Clock Gang*. He was not impressed and remarked, 'My God, how long have you been getting away with this?' The show had been immensely popular in its early years, with long queues waiting patiently every weekday morning to get into the theatre to be part of the fun, but the weekly schedule was grinding and demanding, and ratings began to slip. While Charles Hill's verdict smacked of snobbery and condescension, and was said to have hastened the end of the show, in reality, *The One O'Clock Gang* had probably had its time.

By 1967 STV had retained its franchise and the ITV network had evolved. In return for a schedule of shows made by the big five companies – what eventually became Yorkshire, Granada, Central TV, Thames TV and London Weekend – STV and the other smaller companies paid a fee based on their share of national advertising. This included enormously popular programmes like *Coronation Street*, *Emmerdale Farm* and *Sunday Night at the London Palladium*. STV made a few network programmes, and perhaps the most notable was *Taggart*, a detective series based in Glasgow that ran from 1985 to 2010. It even managed to survive the death of Mark McManus who played the title role. The company was rebranded as Scottish Television in the later 1980s.

In the 1990s the company began to produce many more programmes for the ITV network, expanding its slate of children's series in particular. At one time Scottish Television had four programmes in the children's top ten and three in the top ten drama series. But as ITV consolidated into one company for the whole of England and STV (having bought Grampian TV) remained independent, the amount of network production declined, as did the jobs associated with it. The company's studios and headquarters moved from Cowcaddens across the Clyde to Pacific Quay, and as newspapers did in the face of the internet, the influence and importance of the company has declined markedly in the new broadcasting landscape of multi-channel streaming services.

35

The World's Most Famous Glaswegian

In August 1972, at the Edinburgh Festival Fringe, a new musical play called *The Great Northern Welly Boot Show* attracted a sellout audience of 700 in a makeshift theatre built inside the old Waverley Market on Princes Street. But there was a big problem. Half of those who bought tickets thought the show started at 7.30 p.m., but because of a mistake in an advertisement, the other half thought it began at 8 p.m. That meant the play couldn't start until everyone had arrived, and so what to do about the hundreds of people sitting waiting, no doubt growing fidgety? The co-author of the musical agreed to go out front and entertain the early comers with his banjo and some funny stories until all the latecomers had arrived.

The producer of the play, Kenny Ireland, remembered:

> Billy volunteered to go out front to explain to the audience that there would be a bit of a delay and he said he would do a wee bit of his stuff to keep things going. He'd never performed solo to an audience of more than eighty folkies before, but he blossomed out there. By the time he came off, the place was packed with 700 people laughing at Billy – and he loved it. We didn't get the play on stage until about quarter to nine.

The cast of *The Great Northern Welly Boot Show*, a group of gifted, distinguished actors who would all go on to achieve a great deal, came out from backstage when they heard the waves of laughter. They had mixed feelings. Bill Paterson, later to become a major star in his own right, recalled:

> I had seen him many times before and I've seen him many times since, but I still believe that was his greatest time. He was flying. He loved that big audience, doing his own turn . . . The only problem it gave the rest of us was how to follow him with the play. No one was particularly interested in the show after Billy's performance. It seemed dull by comparison.

That was the moment, on a makeshift stage in Edinburgh, as late-comers took their seats, that the most famous Glaswegian in the world became a star. The Scottish comedy of the *Five-Past Eight* and *One O'Clock Gang* shows was transformed as Connolly mined his lived experience in Glasgow – and it could only have been Glasgow – to make people laugh from Tokyo to Toronto and all points between. The city and its quintessential star would forever be inextricably linked. After his shows, everybody belonged to Glasgow.

But his career was the sum of several accidents. Connolly had been a well-known face on the Scottish folk scene as part of the Humblebums with Gerry Rafferty and Tam Harvey. But when Rafferty left to form the rock group, Stealers Wheel, Connolly looked around for other ways to express his talent. Maybe the theatre would work. He later said:

> I said to Tom Buchan [gifted poet, novelist and playwright], 'Look, I've got a title – "The Great Northern Welly Boot Show". I want it to be about wellies and a sort of thinly

disguised Upper Clyde situation, a work-in in a welly boot factory. And I want to be the shop steward, Big Jimmy Littlejohn. Now I didn't know how to write a proper script, so that an actor could just pick it up and go, "Oh yes. I see. Act One, Scene One." But Tom did. So I wrote all of the songs and he did the script. The whole thing has become a bit of legend, though it was a bit of a disaster to begin with.

Billy Connolly was born in Anderston in Glasgow on 24 November 1942 'on the linoleum' of the kitchen floor of a third-floor tenement flat. His father, also William, was a twenty-three-year-old RAF technician; his mother, Marnie, left the family when Billy was four years old. Later in life, in 2009, his reaction might be seen as surprising:

> I've never felt abandoned by her. My mother was a teenager. My father was in Burma, fighting a bloody war. The Germans were dropping all sorts of crap on the town. We lived at the docks, so that's where all the bombs were happening. She was a teenager with two kids in a slum. A guy comes along and says, 'I love you. Come with me.' Given the choice, I think I'd have gone with him. It looks as though it might all end next Wednesday, from where you're standing. I didn't have an ounce of feelings that she abandoned me. She tried to survive.

Connolly and his sister, Florence, went to live with their father's siblings, Aunt Margaret and Aunt Mona, in a small tenement flat in Partick. After his father returned, his son had to endure years of physical and sexual abuse: 'Sometimes, when father hit me, I flew over the settee backwards in a sitting position. It was fabulous. Just like real flying, except you didn't get a cup of tea or a safety belt or anything'.

Adding a humorous gloss to such terrible experiences is characteristic of Connolly. Between the ages of fourteen and twenty, he lived in Drumchapel, a housing estate outside Glasgow he described as '*in* Glasgow, but just *outside* civilisation'. At the age of sixteen, he began work in the shipyards, as a boilermaker at Alexander Stephen & Son in Linthouse, just west of Govan. It was there that he learned 'how men talked to one another, and how merciless Glasgow humour can be'. In 1965, Connolly left shipbuilding to try to make a career as a folk musician. Danny Kyle was a significant figure in the 1960s revival of interest in traditional music and he recalled: 'I kind of introduced Billy to the folk clubs, such as there were in those days – there were very few . . . We used to go to places like Saturday Late or the Montrose Street Glasgow Folk Club.' When Connolly introduced himself and Tam Harvey at their first Humblebums gig, he said, 'My name's Billy Connolly, and I'm humble. This is Tam Harvey and he's a bum.' Talking later about Gerry Rafferty, he described him as a real musician, someone who really knew and felt music. By his own admission Connolly could learn how to play tunes, but he decided to abandon music and concentrate on what he was really born to do.

It takes a brave man to make comedy out of the Crucifixion of Jesus Christ, but then Connolly was nothing if not brave:

> The door opens . . . crash! And in he comes. The Big Yin . . . wi' the long dress and the casual sandals . . . 'Oot a' mornin' daein' thae miracles. I'm knackered. Gie's a glass o' that wine. Nae kiddin', son, I'm knackered . . . Take a look oot that door. There's nuthin' but deid punters walkin' up and doon, wi' their beds under their airms . . .
>
> Wan o' youse is goin' tae shop me . . . and two big Roman polis is goin' to wheech me right oot o' here and

> into jail . . . And I'm goin' to get up in the mornin' and say first offence, ah'm on to probation, nae bother. But a big Roman is goin' to come intae my cell and say, 'Probationum my arsium . . .'

On 15 February 1975, only two and a half years after he had delighted audiences at *The Great Northern Welly Boot Show*, Connolly appeared on *The Michael Parkinson Show*. Talking about wellies, of course, and tyrannical teachers forcing him to sing 'Mairi's Wedding', he made his life experiences into priceless comedy, all of it delivered in an unaltered Glasgow accent. That appearance established Connolly in Britain, but the universal nature of his themes took him to international stardom. He is without doubt one of the greatest comedians of all time, but that is a description that misleads. Connolly has never told set-piece jokes; his humour comes from acute observation and a realisation that the particular – particular to Glasgow, to its shipyards and tenements – can be seen as universal, recognisable across the planet. But he has never lost his pride in his origins. In an appearance soon after the 2007 terrorist attack on Glasgow Airport, he said proudly, 'That's Glasgow. That's where I come from.'

36

Miles Better

In 1983 the opening of the Burrell Collection in Glasgow led the national news on BBC and ITV. It made a welcome change from industrial woes, reports of violence or scenes of bleak housing estates as the tower blocks of the 1960s tumbled. In 1988 the Glasgow Garden Festival opened on a reclaimed industrial site on the south bank of the Clyde and it attracted a record 4.1 million visitors. Two years later Glasgow was named as the European Capital of Culture. Not Edinburgh – Glasgow. And arguably the city's crowning glory was the Commonwealth Games held in 2014.

The undeniable renaissance of modern Glasgow owes a great deal to two men: Michael Kelly, Lord Provost from 1980 to 1984, and John Struthers, who ran one of the most successful independent advertising agencies in the west of Scotland. Both were much impressed by the I Love New York campaign of 1977 which turned around perceptions – and the fortunes – of that great but often embattled city. Could the same sort of thing be done for Glasgow albeit on a much smaller budget?

John Struthers had worked with the Scottish Health Education Group on an anti-smoking campaign, and when he read that Michael Kelly had ambitions to make Glasgow a no-smoking city, he offered his services. When the two men met over a cup of coffee, they agreed that there should be a campaign to do more than ban smoking; it should aim to improve the image of Glasgow after decades of negative publicity and economic retreat. Kelly and Struthers wanted nothing less than Glasgow to feel good about itself, for all that Victorian self-confidence to return to the banks of the Clyde.

On a train trip to London with his fourteen-year-old son, Mark, they both doodled and discussed what a campaign might look like. On a bit of paper one of them wrote 'Glasgow's Miles Better'. Now that they had a tagline, the campaign symbol also needed to be positive – but also cheery, cheeky – so that it fitted with perceptions of the city and its people. It turned out that the right symbol already existed. It was to be the round, yellow, beaming figure of Mr Happy from the Mister Men series of children's books. It helped a great deal with copyright that Roger Hargreaves, the creator of the series, was an old friend of John Struthers.

While Glasgow could not afford the sums spent by New York, cash was raised from the city of Glasgow, the Scottish Development Agency and contributions from local businesses. The whole campaign may have cost less than £400,000, an amazing bargain when its impact is taken into account.

Billy Connolly, Lulu and other famous showbiz names were happy to be involved in the launch of Glasgow's Miles Better in June 1983. Perhaps because it was so different from messages in the past, so positive, so surprising and so intriguing, the campaign took off in a way that amazed everyone involved. The slogan began to be quoted worldwide, and there were sightings of stickers in the Himalayas and reports that Mr Happy had appeared in towns thousands of miles east of Moscow – Moscow, Russia, not East Ayrshire. For much of the 1980s, far longer than comparable initiatives, his beaming yellow face seemed to be everywhere: on buses, railway bridges, umbrellas, car stickers and T-shirts. All of which was helped along by Glasgow's perennial rival to the east when Edinburgh City Council banned the Glasgow slogan from their buses. Glasgow had wanted to take advantage of the International Festival and the Fringe by advertising their campaign on six Edinburgh buses. But the council wasn't having it. So Glasgow passed the story along to the world's press, conveniently gathered in the city for the festival, and even the *Wall Street Journal* ran it. Edinburgh ended up with a red face while Glasgow's councillors rubbed their hands at all the free publicity the Miles Better campaign was getting. It looked like Glasgow was behaving Miles Better than Edinburgh. Because it was.

Of course, Scotland being snarky Scotland, it didn't take long for other versions of the slogan to appear: Glasgow's Miles Better Than What? Glasgow's Miles Better Than Calcutta and Bogota, Glasgow's Miles Better Than It Used to Be – But It's Still Got a Long Way to Go. All good grist to the mill, and vindication for John Struther's advertising nous in keeping the proposition open as well as positive.

None of the mickey-taking, or the Edinburgh rivalry, mattered very much. In the opinion of one expert the campaign 'is to be considered one of the best city promotions ever mounted by any British city. It put a smile on a city that was both down on its heels and negatively perceived.' Harry Diamond was the head of the city's PR operations at the time. In his well-titled book, *Can You Get My Name in the Papers?*, he described the campaign as a stellar success. 'There was a lot happening in the city at that time and we made lots of things happen . . . Success in anything brings its rewards, it makes you feel you are doing a worthwhile job. There was a great deal of satisfaction.'

Michael Kelly later told the BBC that the legacy of the Glasgow's Miles Better campaign was 'a permanent change in attitude towards Glasgow, exposing the reality rather than the distorted image people had . . . We changed the media's perception of the city. People began to look at it in a proper light and were able to make economic decisions based on that, so we got investment, we got employment.' Kelly went on to found his own PR agency, Michael Kelly Associates, and also to be elected rector of Glasgow University. But John Struthers, the man who devised the famous slogan (with help from his son), sadly suffered from years of ill health and died in 2001. There can be no doubt that he made a huge and lasting contribution to his native city.

37

Honoured Servants of the People

Late on the night of 20 November 1922, a huge crowd gathered in St Enoch Square, spilling into the adjacent streets. Many had marched behind banners from all over Glasgow. The words of William Blake rang out as James Houston conducted the William Morris Choir and led perhaps 80,000 people to sing 'Jerusalem':

> I will not cease from Mental Fight,
> Nor shall my sword sleep in my hand:
> Till we have built Jerusalem,
> In Englands green & pleasant Land.

Lit by the arc lamps above the station façade, two red flags fluttered and glowed in the night wind. The choir sang Psalm 124 and the crowd joined them:

> Now Israel
>   may say, and that truly,
> If that the Lord
>   had not our cause maintain'd;
> If that the Lord
>   had not our right sustain'd,
> When cruel men
>   against us furiously

Rose up in wrath,
        to make of us their prey;

More like a massed outdoor conventicle from the seventeenth century and the time of the Covenanters than a political rally, those gathered in the square believed themselves present at a time of great and long overdue change. The men they had come to send off would 'abjure vanity and self-aggrandisment, recognising that they are the honoured servants of the people and that their only righteous purpose is to promote the welfare of their fellow citizens and the wellbeing of mankind'.

In the general election of 1922, Labour swept to power in Glasgow and in the mining and industrial communities around the city. Eighteen new MPs would leave on the night mail train for London to represent the mass of voters who had supported them. Mechanics, joiners, miners, a hairdresser had all won seats, and the great Tom Johnston had won West Stirlingshire. But the core leaders, the MPs who became known as the Clyde Brigade, were David Kirkwood and John Wheatley (veterans of the 1919 riot in George Square), George Buchanan, Campbell Stephen and, perhaps the most significant figure of them all, James Maxton.

At a time when platform oratory mattered, especially in front of large crowds – and there had been none larger than the crowd that gathered on 20 November – James Maxton was a gifted, magnetic speaker. Tall, cadaverously thin and with a lick of long, lank hair tucked behind one ear, he preached peaceful revolution – and, as one journalist commented, he looked like it. When Maxton climbed onto the platform at St Enoch Square, his back was bruised from slapping and his hands ached from being vigorously and repeatedly shaken. He began, as often, with humour. It had been more difficult, he said, to get to St Enoch Station than to the House of Commons. Andrew Bonar Law, the new prime minister, had held on to his Glasgow Central seat by a whisker and had campaigned with the slogan, 'Peace and Tranquillity', taken from a popular hymn. Maxton paraphrased it for the crowd:

Bonar, seek not yet repose,
Cast the dream of rest away:
Thou art in the midst of foes –
Watch and pray.

'Rely on us,' said Maxton to the crowd, 'as we rely on you.' And to reassure them on the impact that the small group of Glasgow MPs might have relative to the entire number of MPs in other parties, he went on: 'People talk about the atmosphere of the House of Commons getting the better of the Labour men, but they will see the atmosphere of the Clyde getting the better of the House of Commons.'

With the cheers of the crowd ringing in their ears, the new MPs boarded the night train to try to win a better future for all of Glasgow's people and those working men and women who lived around the city.

James Maxton and his colleagues were only the first in a long line of distinguished politicians who represented constituencies in Glasgow. Born into a comfortably well-off Edinburgh family and dux of the private school Edinburgh Academy, Geoff Shaw became an unlikely Labour politician, a man whom many believed would become the first First Minister of a devolved Scottish Parliament.

After completing his National Service in the Royal Navy, Shaw responded to a call to become a minister and studied divinity at Edinburgh University. With four similarly minded friends, he formed a partnership in Glasgow that became known as the Gorbals Group. It was a radical attempt at social gospel ministry. Instead of living in a manse and being in charge of a parish, Shaw and his friends lived in the tenements of what was still one of the worst slums in Europe. They held open house and shared worship, money and food among themselves. Jimmy Boyle, the one-time gangster from the 1960s who made a new life as an author and sculptor, remarked that 'never have I heard of people being let down by Geoff Shaw'.

In 1970 Shaw was elected to Glasgow Corporation for the ward of Govanhill. When local government was reorganised in 1974 and the vast Strathclyde Region (named after the old kingdom based at Govan) was created, Geoff Shaw became its first convener. Soon afterwards, the Labour Government began to formulate legislation to bring a Scottish Assembly into being, and an enabling act was passed in 1978. But it was already too late. Geoff Shaw had died of a heart attack on 28 April 1978. Twenty years later, on the brink of more legislation that would succeed in bringing about a Scottish Parliament, an article appeared in the *Herald*:

> At the time of Geoff Shaw's death, it looked as if Scotland was on the brink of achieving Home Rule. And the name on many people's lips as the obvious candidate for first Scottish Premier was the Rev. Geoffrey Mackintosh Shaw. The *Glasgow Evening Times* had run an article on its front page, under the banner headline, 'Who will be Scotland's first Prime Minister?' They profiled various candidates, and put their money on Shaw.

In 1998 there was no point in going to the betting shop. If elected, Donald Dewar, the MP for Glasgow Anniesland, would become Scotland's First Minister. And so it came to pass. On 1 July 1999, he began his speech at the opening session of the new Scottish Parliament by quoting the first line of the Scotland Act that had brought it into being:

> 'There shall be a Scottish Parliament.' Through long years, those words were first a hope, then a belief, then a promise. Now they are a reality. This is a moment anchored in our history . . . This is about more than our politics and our laws. This is about who we are, how we carry ourselves. In the quiet moments today, we might hear some echoes from the past:
>
> The shout of the welder in the din of the great Clyde shipyards:
>
> The speak of the Mearns, with its soul in the land;
>
> The discourse of the enlightenment, when Edinburgh and Glasgow were a light held to the intellectual life of Europe;
>
> The wild cry of the Great Pipes;
>
> And back to the distant cries of the battles of Bruce and Wallace.
>
> The past is part of us. But today there is a new voice in the land, the voice of a democratic parliament. A voice to shape Scotland, a voice for the future.

Sadly, like Geoff Shaw, Donald Dewar died young, at only sixty-three, on 11 October 2000.

38

Nova Glasgow

In 1688 the first commercial quay on the Clyde was built at Brumelaw, the Broomielaw, where bushes of yellow-flowering broom once grew by the waterside. In the early eighteenth century, it became a central part of Glasgow's harbour facilities, where ships cast off to begin voyages across oceans to other continents, spending weeks and months at sea. In the twentieth century, according to 'The Song Of The Clyde', made famous by Kenneth McKellar:

> There's Paw an' Maw at Glasgow Broomielaw,
> They're goin' 'doon the water' for 'the Fair'.
> There's Bob an' Mary on the Govan Ferry
> Wishin' jet propulsion could be there.
> There's steamers cruisin', and there's buddies snoozin',
> And there's laddies fishin' frae the pier;
> An' Paw's perspirin', very near expirin',
> As he rows a boat frae there to here.

By the twenty-first century, the Broomielaw had become the centre of a very different kind of traffic, one that took seconds to complete rather than weeks or months: the movement of money. Glaswegians who enjoy a little sceptical self-deprecation, and few don't, have started calling it 'Wall Street on Clyde', or 'Scotland's Square Kilometre'. What they mean is that chunk of central Glasgow that is bounded in the east by the King George V Bridge, in the west by the motorway traffic thundering over the Kingston Bridge, in the north by St Vincent Street and on the south bank of the Clyde by Morrison Street.

This is the geography of Glasgow's financial sector, and it is booming. The city has been climbing up the ranks of the world's financial sectors until it now occupies fifty-third place, up thirty-one since 2019. In Britain, only London and Edinburgh are ranked ahead of Glasgow. According to Sandy Begbie of Scottish Financial Enterprise, this is also good for the whole of Scotland. Having two of the UK's top financial centres only forty miles apart, more or less cheek by jowl, whatever the inter-city rivalries, makes them 'part of the same ecosystem, closely connected and easily accessible to one another'. Wisely, in an age of virtual meetings, he is not discounting the value of physical, face-to-face exchanges. And there is a new booster organisation to underpin all this expansion: the International Financial Services District. It is supported by Glasgow City Council, the Scottish Government, the Glasgow Chamber of Commerce and all the city's universities and colleges. The IFSD is not shy about its presence and role, and its banners hang from lampposts on the streets of Wall Street on Clyde.

An impressive list of companies now operate out of Glasgow. They include branches of J. P. Morgan, BNP Paribas, Lloyds Bank, Credit Suisse, BDO Global, HSBC, Tesco Bank, Direct Line, Scottish Widows, NFU Mutual and others. Not all of them manage money or insurance. The German industrial giant Siemens is there, as is First Data Corporation, the Weir Group (almost certainly the longest-established manufacturer in Glasgow to be represented), BT, the British Steel Pension Fund and Atkins, the noted civil engineering company. Government is also represented in what is also sometimes called Nova Glasgow. In the darkened glass towers of Atlantic Square sit the Scottish headquarters of the Cabinet Office and HMRC. On the Broomielaw is the Scottish Government's Glasgow office.

No company actually makes or builds anything on this stretch of the river, the hammers no longer ding-dong in the old song of the Clyde, but what was a very neglected area has been regenerated over a short period. The south bank in particular was once dismal but is now a pleasant area of cityscape with shiny new buildings and a tree-lined walkway along the river. Perhaps, one day, broom will be planted. The International Financial Services District was linked in 2009 by the opening of the Squiggly Bridge, also marked on city maps as the Tradeston Bridge. For pedestrians and cyclists only, the span is curved in an S-shape so that the bridge can be extended and more easily allow boats to pass underneath. S, allegedly, stands for Squiggly. The southern edge of the district is dominated by the eight-storey towers of the European headquarters of Barclays Bank and the head office of the Student Loan Company.

Beyond the Kingston Bridge, on the south side of the river, are the offices and studios of two distinguished migrants, both of them having moved from sites in the city centre. STV's large studios next to the Theatre Royal were thought to be unnecessary in the twenty-first century television landscape, and so the company moved to Pacific Quay to a new headquarters in the kind of glass-boxes-with-parking that have become popular in parts of modern Glasgow. The BBC has also fled the city centre from its buildings that were partly designed by Charles Rennie Mackintosh in Queen Margaret Drive, near the Botanic Garden. The more recent and anonymous building next door to it was where the appalling *White Heather Club* was produced in the 1960s.

Further west stand three modern buildings on the site of Prince's Dock. It was initially filled in to become the venue for the 1988 Garden Festival. The three buildings make up the Glasgow Science Centre, opened by Queen Elizabeth II in May 2001. The Science Mall is shaped like the upside-down hull of a ship, which is appropriate. Built in 2018, it was the first in Scotland to be clad in titanium. And possibly the last. It leaked and had to be reclad in 2023 with stainless-steel shingles. Inside are three levels that include interactive scientific fun for schoolchildren and a planetarium, a spectacular, full-dome digital projection system that takes people on virtual journeys through space.

The huge silver globe next door is an IMAX cinema. When it opened to the public in 2000, it was the first of its kind in Scotland, and 370 people enjoyed its vast screens and immersive sound. Perhaps the most innovative building is the Glasgow Tower, which was completed in 2001 and designed by Richard Horden and Buro Happold. At 417 feet, it is the highest building in Glasgow and the highest freestanding building in Scotland, the equivalent of a stack of thirty double-decker buses. It was originally to be placed in St Enoch Square in the middle of the old city, but common sense prevailed, and it replaced the Clydesdale Bank Tower set up for the Garden Festival. At the top is a revolving observatory served by two lifts (which take only twenty-five seconds to reach the top) and a less attractive emergency staircase of 523 steps. It is a complex structure that has proved to be prone to problems, and the council were forced to sue the (now defunct) builders, Carillon, over the quality of some of their construction. But when it all works, the view from the top is stunning. It is the only structure in the world capable of rotating 360 degrees into the prevailing western winds, and it holds the Guinness World Record for the tallest, fully rotating freestanding structure in the world. Clearly, Glasgow's Miles Higher.

Directly opposite all that science is show business, and a lot of it. On the other bank of the Clyde is the vast building originally known as the Scottish Exhibition and Conference Centre, now the Scottish Event Campus. The biggest component in this cluster of massive exhibition/entertainment facilities opened in 1985 and was unceremoniously labelled 'The Big Red Shed'. Until it was painted grey in 1997. It occupies sixty-four acres, most of it car parking, and it has its own station (Exhibition Centre) on the Argyle Line. To the south is the Armadillo, so called because it looks like a giant version of the scaly South American animal. Started in 1995 and completed in 1997, it was designed by the English architects (known as starchitects) Foster & Partners, and it seats 3,000. Accused of creating a Glaswegian version of the Sydney Opera House, Norman Foster quoted the city's shipbuilding heritage and claimed its shape was inspired by 'interlocking ships' hulls'. The Armadillo is connected by passageways to the SEC and the nearby Crowne Plaza Hotel, presumably so that performing celebrities can scuttle back to their hotel without being harassed by Glaswegian (and other) fans. Also attached to the SEC is the OVO Hydro, a circular auditorium that began life in 2014 as the Scottish Hydro Arena and changed its name when the company was taken over in 2021 by OVO Energy. Also designed by Foster & Partners, its capacity is vast at 14,300, and it has become an irresistible venue for the very biggest touring acts.

Glasgow's locomotive and shipbuilding past is remembered by yet another starchitect only a few hundred yards west of the Scottish Event Campus. Designed by the Iraqi-born British architect, the late Zaha Hadid, the Glasgow Riverside Museum on Pointhouse Quay is the successor to the old

Transport Museum that used to be in the Kelvin Hall. It opened in 2011, and in 2013 this stunning building was deservedly voted the European Museum of the Year. Most impressive is the collection of 250 models of 200 years of Clyde-built ships, ranging from Bell's paddle steamer, *Comet*, of 1812 to the battleships HMS *Hood* and HMS *Howe* to the three Queens, *Mary*, *Elizabeth* and the *QE2*. There are also Argyll and Arrol-Johnston motor cars, Scottish-built Hillman Imps and Chrysler Sunbeams, a beautiful steam locomotive from the North British Locomotive Company of Springburn, trams, buses and a model of the old St Enoch Station where the Red Clyde MPs were waved off.

This sprawling, impressive network of performance spaces and museums, as well as the financial district, is linked by a series of new bridges across the Clyde: the Millennium and Bell's footbridges, the Squinty Bridge and the Squiggly Bridge and the Clyde Arc vehicular bridge. These new attractions and facilities are fed and watered by three- and four-star hotels: the Crowne Plaza, the Hilton Garden Inn, the Radisson, the Moxy, the Campanile and a Premier Inn.

Instead of mourning the passing of the mighty manufacturing industries that were once the song of the Clyde, Glasgow has remade its industrial past to fit into what is now the world's greatest industry, and that is tourism.

Oh, the River Clyde, the wonderful Clyde,
The name of it thrills me and fills me with pride.

And so it should.

39

Envoi

'That's f****** Pavarotti, by the way.'

Having been cut up at the junction of Hope Street and St Vincent Street, my taxi driver's response was to turn up his dashboard cassette machine as it played 'Nessun Dorma' and wind down his window to abuse the motorist who had pushed out in front of him. It was an old Glasgow response but with a new theme. This scene took place as I sat in the back, running late on my way from STV's studios to the M8 and Glasgow Airport. It was the summer of 1990, the high summer of the European City of Culture. It was an accolade that not only resonated with my taxi driver but could also serve as a rebuke to someone who was somehow letting the city down, pal. I had been to the SECC, having taken a party of London media folk (including the barefoot singer Sandie Shaw, who wore a striking pair of sequined cycle pants, and her husband, Nik Powell, the film producer) to see Luciano Pavarotti's solo concert on 16 May 1990. In the moment's silence before the orchestra struck up and he began to sing, a lone voice rang out from the packed auditorium. 'Go, big man!'

After the stunning, transformative success of the Miles Better campaign, Glasgow purred and basked in the glow of 1990. London media folk did not have to be persuaded to come to the city. It had come to rival, and in some ways surpass, Edinburgh in August, as the only place in Britain that could shift the cultural focus of the country decisively away from London. And Big Lucy's concert was proof, certainly for one taxi driver.

After six years running the Edinburgh Festival Fringe, I had come to work in Glasgow as STV's Arts Correspondent. I was attached to the *Scotland Today* newsroom, hired to do stories on the cultural life of Central Scotland, Monday to Friday, and, in particular, feature what was happening in Glasgow. The more polite of my colleagues, known as the Newsroom Bears, raised an eyebrow. The less polite, peering at me through the fug of cigarette smoke, commented, 'Culture? What f****** culture? This is Glesca.'

I made my nervous debut on the evening news programme with the announcement of a new festival. Mayfest arose from the Scottish Trades Union-organised May Day Parades, and I was to interview the organiser. It all started badly when the *Scotland Today* host introduced me to our million-plus viewers as 'the Darts Correspondent'. The format was a live interview with the woman who would run the festival. This was to take place on two sofas set at right angles in the studio. And it was only the first of two items in that evening's programme for the Darts Correspondent. Because there was no gap in the running order to get in my second item, an interview with a distinguished actor about his new autobiography, he sat next to the lady from Mayfest, but out of shot. Except he didn't stay there. Halfway through the first interview, he leaned across and, as she was talking to me, kissed the woman on the cheek. All hell broke loose. I had to introduce him. And then at the end of a brief tour around his career, the actor announced, possibly after having had a sherry or two in the green room before we went on air, that he had always wanted to do the weather forecast, the next item. I only just managed to restrain him.

Life at STV improved. As Michael Kelly and John Struthers worked their PR magic, Glasgow turned out to need a Darts Correspondent after all. I made a film for Channel 4 about the Burrell Collection, another about Charles Rennie Mackintosh that starred Paisley-born Tom Conti and his wife Kara, and the TV station began to reflect the changes that were clearly taking place, and quickly. The Newsroom Bears began to look like men from the past as the fug of blue cigarette smoke cleared, their clacking typewriters gave way to screens, and videotape replaced film. I made a short film about a marching band of young people based in Springburn. I'd come to understand Glasgow's love affair with the USA – perhaps an unconscious harking back to the age of the Tobacco Lords, the building of ships that crossed the Atlantic and the waves of emigration. It was heart-warming to watch these young people high-stepping to American music. Glasgow had long looked to the west, and only occasionally over its shoulder to hoity-toity Edinburgh and the east.

In 1989 I was appointed Director of Programmes as STV applied for the renewal of its franchise. We decided that the company would embrace the changing face of the city and our wider region in our local programming as well as what we made for the ITV network. That in turn led to a huge raft of new offers to the audience. The government had asked rival bidders for the ITV franchises to offer cash for their licences, and providing that the proposed programming met reasonable standards, the highest bid would win. At STV we decided to offer only £2,000, the minimum annual payment to the Treasury, but spend a great deal of cash in expanding and enhancing our regional programmes. These reflected not only the changes in Glasgow but also Edinburgh, the Lothians, Fife, parts of the Highlands and Ayrshire. During the 1980s and 1990s, Glasgow had come to offer so much more that only the annual Edinburgh Festival and Fringe could attract attention away from what was happening on the banks of the Clyde.

Looking back now, the speed of all that change was remarkable. But not surprising. Cultural reinvention is a long tradition in Glasgow. Change was never something Glaswegians recoiled from or resisted – right across the city. 'That's f****** Pavarotti, by the way' can be added to John Smeaton's defiance and definition of identity under duress. Both men loved the city with a passion and understood its unique character.

Further Reading

This should read Further Clicking. More and more as I research my books, I find myself using the vast, labyrinthine resources of the internet to discover new material. Since the story of Glasgow is heavily weighted to the modern period, there are real nuggets to be found amongst the dross: film footage of the inventor, George Bennie, and his monorail, mass meetings of workers in George Square in 1919 and John Grierson's Oscar-winning film, *Seawards the Great Ships*, can all be seen after a minimum of mouse-clicks.

A distinguished journalist, my old friend George Rosie, added a great deal from the world of newspapers he knows so well, including a brilliant summary of Billy Connolly riffing on Christ's crucifixion. Here are some literary sources that were helpful as well as some other useful books on the city.

Craig, Maggie, *When the Clyde Ran Red: A Social History of Red Clydeside*, Edinburgh 2018

Devine T.M., *The Scottish Nation*, London 2012

Dudgeon, Piers, *Our Glasgow: Memories of Life in Disappearing Britain*, London 2010

Foreman, Carol, *Lost Glasgow*, Edinburgh 2019

Fry, Michael, *Glasgow: A History of the City*, London 2017

Fry, Michael, *The Scottish Empire*, Edinburgh 2001

Glasser, Ralph, *Growing Up in the Gorbals*, Edinburgh 2006

Hall, Derek, Burgess, *Merchant and Priest: The Medieval Burgh Town*, Edinburgh 2002

Hanley, Clifford, *Dancing in the Streets*, Edinburgh 2024

Moffat, Alistair, *Scotland: A History from Earliest Times*, Edinburgh, 2017

Moore, John, *The Clyde; Mapping the River*, Edinburgh 2017

Moore, John, *Glasgow: Mapping the City*, Edinburgh 2015

Paterson, Bill, *Tales from the Back Green*, London 2008

Smout, T.C., *A Century of the Scottish People*, London 2010

Taylor, Alan (ed.), *Glasgow: The Autobiography*, Edinburgh 2024

Acknowledgements

No one I know has a sharper eye for a good story than George Rosie. Mainly in television, we have worked together for more than forty years and in all that time George's judgment has been gimlet-sharp and his joy in a good yarn undimmed. We made many great programmes together, culminating in George winning a BAFTA in 1999 for his film on the tenth anniversary of the Lockerbie disaster. He also had a huge role in drawing together the material for this book, constantly seeing things I would have missed. And we had a lot of fun doing it. Alison Rae copy-edited *Glasgow: A New History* with great care and much good humour, getting the balance of material just so. One day, the three of us may celebrate with a cup of tea and a Tunnock's Caramel Wafer, or two. Many thanks to both.

Index

ALSO AVAILABLE BY ALISTAIR MOFFAT

To See Ourselves: A Personal History of Scotland Since 1950

Since the end of the Second World War, life in Scotland has changed at breakneck speed and is now entirely different from what it was like when Alistair Moffat grew up in the Border town of Kelso in the 1950s. At that time the rhythm of daily life, which had remained constant for generations, was about to change in the most unimaginable ways.

This is a book about those changes – many of which have been dizzying and disorientating – and how they have affected each and every one of us. The main themes – from health, housing and education to religion, sport, the media and politics – are all viewed through the lens of personal experience. Moffat's own recollections of big events and small, together with other eyewitness accounts, bring these decades alive in a way that no ordinary history can, with a directness and poignancy that underlines how much has been gained – and how much lost.

Edinburgh: A New History

From prehistory to the present day, the story of Edinburgh is packed with incident and drama. As Scotland's capital since the fifteenth century, the city has witnessed many of the key events which have shaped the nation.

But Edinburgh has always been much more than a political centre. During the Enlightenment it was one of the intellectual powerhouses of Europe, and in the twentieth century it became the arts capital of the world with the founding of its many festivals. Finance, religion, education, sport and industry are also important parts of the story.

Alistair Moffat explores these themes and many more, showing how the city has grown, changed and adapted over the centuries. He introduces Edinburgh's famous places and people – including monarchs, murderers, writers and philosophers – as well as the ordinary citizens who have contributed so much to the life of one of the world's best-loved cities.

The Highlands and Islands of Scotland: A New History

This is the story of the Highlands and Islands of Scotland as it has never been told before. From the formation of the landscape millions of years ago to the twenty-first century, it brings to life the events and the people who have shaped Highland history. Picts, Romans, Irish missionaries, Vikings, Jacobites and the flood of emigrants who left to forge new lives abroad are just some of the important players in the drama. As he paints the bigger picture, Alistair Moffat also introduces many key aspects of Highland culture and explores the experience of ordinary Highlanders and Islanders over thousands of years.

'A splendid and thoroughly enjoyable book; one from which most of us can surely learn a lot. I would advise reading it straight through, then returning to dip in again and again'
The Scotsman

'A very personal history, richly informative and sparkling with detail'
Country Life

'Not simply a history of kings, queens and nobles . . . Throw in Moffat's uncanny ability to root out neatly illustrative gems from obscure primary sources, plus his easy and engaging writing style, and the end result is a book which undoubtedly adds to the sum of our knowledge'
Scottish Field

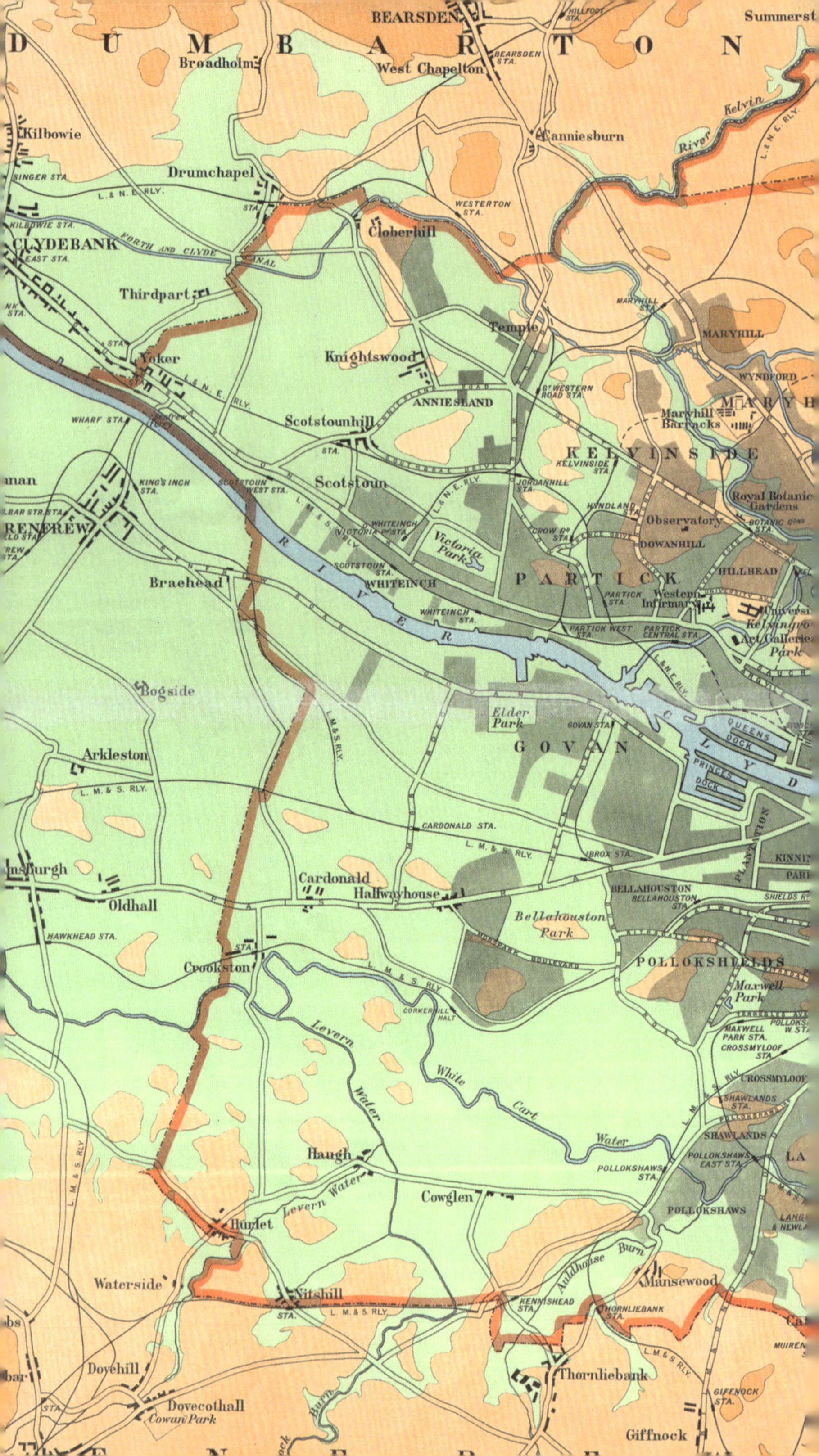

DUMBARTON
BEARSDEN
Summerston
Broadholm
West Chapelton
BEARSDEN STA.
HILLFOOT STA.
Kilbowie
Canniesburn
River Kelvin
L. & N. E. RLY.
Drumchapel
SINGER STA.
WESTERTON STA.
KILBOWIE STA.
FORTH AND CLYDE CANAL
CLYDEBANK
EAST STA.
Cloberhill
Thirdpart
MARYHILL STA.
MARYHILL
Temple
Yoker
Knightswood
WYNDFORD
ANNIESLAND
GT WESTERN ROAD STA.
WHARF STA.
Scotstounhill
Maryhill Barracks
KELVINSIDE
KELVINSIDE STA.
KING'S INCH STA.
Scotstoun
SCOTSTOUN WEST STA.
JORDANHILL STA.
Royal Botanic Gardens
RENFREW
HYNDLAND STA.
Observatory
VICTORIA PK STA.
Victoria Park
CROW RD STA.
DOWANHILL
BOTANIC GDNS STA.
RIVER
SCOTSTOUN STA.
WHITEINCH
PARTICK
HILLHEAD
Braehead
PARTICK STA.
Western Infirmary
WHITEINCH STA.
PARTICK WEST STA.
PARTICK CENTRAL STA.
Art Galleries
Bogside
L.M.& S. RLY.
Elder Park
GOVAN STA.
GOVAN
QUEENS DOCK
CLYDE
PRINCES DOCK
Arkleston
L. M. & S. RLY.
CARDONALD STA.
PLANTATION
IBROX STA.
Cardonald
Halfwayhouse
BELLAHOUSTON
BELLAHOUSTON STA.
Oldhall
Bellahouston Park
HAWKHEAD STA.
STA.
Crookston
POLLOKSHIELDS
Maxwell Park
CORKERHILL HALT
Levern Water
MAXWELL PARK STA.
CROSSMYLOOF STA.
White Cart Water
CROSSMYLOOF
SHAWLANDS STA.
SHAWLANDS
Haugh
POLLOKSHAWS STA.
POLLOKSHAWS EAST STA.
Cowglen
Levern Water
POLLOKSHAWS
Hurlet
Auldhouse Burn
Waterside
Mansewood
Nitshill
STA.
KENNISHEAD STA.
THORNLIEBANK STA.
Dovehill
Thornliebank
Dovecothall
Cowan Park
GIFFNOCK STA.
Giffnock